DOG
TRAINING HANDBOOK

A 10–WEEK TRAINING COURSE

STELLA SMYTH & SALLY BERGH-ROOSE

Sterling Publishing Co., Inc.
New York

DEDICATION

With thanks to all the wonderful dog trainers past and present from whom we have learned so much, but especially to Brenda, who made us pay attention!

This book was created by KINSEY & Harrison for HarperCollins*Publishers* Limited.

Photography by Tracy Morgan Animal Photography

Note: Dogs obviously come in both sexes, but to simplify our training message we have used "he" rather than "he/she" or "it" when referring to any dog.

Library of Congress-in-Publication Data Available

10 9 8 7 6 5 4 3 2 1

Published in 2002 by
Sterling Publishing Co., Inc.
387 Park Avenue South
New York, NY 10016
First published by
HarperCollins*Publishers*
77–85 Fulham Palace Road
Hammersmith, London W6 8JB
© HarperCollins*Publishers* Ltd, 2001
Distributed in Canada by
Sterling Publishing
C/o Canadian Manda Group
One Atlantic Avenue, Suite 105
Toronto, Ontario, M6K 3E7

Color reproduction by
Colorscan, Singapore
Printed in Hong Kong

Sterling ISBN 1-4027-0197-7

CON

TENTS

Introduction

This book is intended to be a basic beginners' guide to training your dog step by step. We feel it is a shame that so many people obtain their dog or puppy and only then, or later when a problem occurs, do they worry about training. Many people also wait until the dog is six months old before seriously thinking about doing some form of training, as historically this was considered the norm. These days we are a lot more enlightened and realize the vast benefits of socializing puppies and channeling their behavior at an early age.

Praise and Reward

Our training methods are based on being kind to the dog, with the emphasis on praise and reward.

This is designed to be a hands-on manual that can be of benefit to owners with dogs of any age or breed. One of the problems we have found over many years in our training classes is the clumsy and awkward way in which owners handle their dogs, especially when the dog is on the lead. Far too often the dogs are pushed and pulled around and given a multitude of conflicting signals that bear no relation to the owner's verbal requests. This leads to frustration for the owner and total confusion for the dog.

In this book we aim to show our techniques, which we have refined over years of practice, to help owners achieve smoother handling of their dogs. The training methods illustrated have been used with our own dogs, which have gone on to do competition work as well as being happy family pets. Between us over the last 25 years we have had a selection of dogs, from working sheepdogs to German Shepherds, Labradors, and Australian Cattle Dogs. They have joined us at varying ages – some carefully selected as puppies, others older who came into our lives by chance – but all of them loved dearly and all responded successfully to the same simple methods we present here.

Size Does Matter

The size of the dog frequently has a bearing on owners' attitudes to training. Small dogs are generally considered to be much less of a problem, whether they be adult or puppy, as they are usually unceremoniously picked up at the first hint of trouble. This does not solve any problems, it just changes them. Many owners of small dogs tend to tolerate their dog's bad behavior, possibly because they still equate them with being puppies because of their size.

Puppies of large and giant breeds tend to have the opposite problem. They become very large at a young age and because of their large size their owners often expect too much of them – yet mentally they are still babies.

Owners' Responsibilities

Anyone who owns a dog has a responsibility to the dog, themselves, and society in general: to care for it to the best of their ability and prevent it from being a nuisance. So training is critical. Being firm, however, does not mean that your dog will not to love you. In fact, the opposite is the case: terrible mental suffering can be caused to the dog who has no clear ground rules. The increase in mutual love and respect that can be developed during training is enormous. If this book helps you to appreciate that fact, then it will have been worthwhile.

CHAPTER ONE WHY TRAIN YOUR DOG?

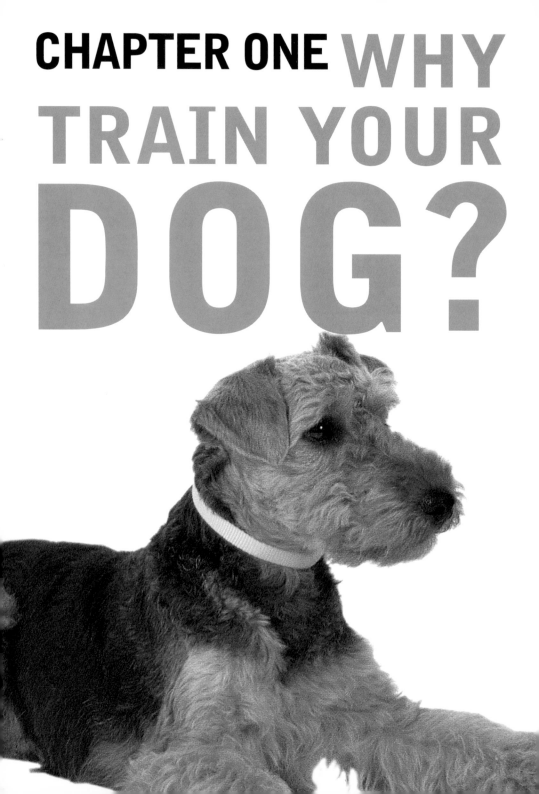

Reasons for Training

Unruly dogs are like unruly children – they are a menace to have around. Everyone wants a dog that fits in with their lifestyle and is a pleasure to be with. Unfortunately, puppies are not born ready-trained and some effort has to be put in to achieve that comfortable relationship.

We are often asked "What is acceptable behavior?" The answer is whatever is acceptable to the owner. One person may be happy to have the dog (or dogs) sleep on the end of their bed – another would be horrified and find this quite unacceptable. The proviso to this is that if the dog's behavior is unacceptable to other people then the owner may have a problem. Very few people will tolerate indiscriminate fouling, excessive noise, or intractable behavior from other people's animals.

Sadly, rescue kennels are always full to overflowing with dogs looking for a new home. While some are in rescue for genuine reasons, a large number are there because the relationship between dog and family has broken down, or not reached the family's expectations. In many cases this could have been prevented by proper training.

Training Throughout the Day

Dog training should not be limited to half an hour a day, and your dog left to his own devices for the other twenty three and a half hours. The verbal commands we teach should be useful on many occasions throughout the day, for example STAND for grooming or at the vet, or SIT to have the collar and lead put on, or before crossing the road or getting into or out of the car. Remember, an out-of-control dog is a danger to himself and to others.

Mutual Benefit

Both you and your dog can benefit from the mental stimulation of training sessions. At the same time, your one-to-one relationship with your dog will be strengthened as both of you learn to communicate with each other. Successful training is a great confidence booster for all dogs and owners, especially those with a shy and reserved nature.

Defining the Boundaries

Dogs are pack animals and although it is more important to some dogs than others, they will be more emotionally stable and secure if the boundaries of acceptable behavior within the family "pack" have been made clear. This sounds very rigid but it need not be; it is no more severe than insisting your children be well-mannered. Most owners derive great pleasure from having others admire their well-behaved dog.

Dog Training Should Be Fun

For whatever reason you decide to get a dog; you should strive to enjoy a strong companionship with him so that, above all, dog training will be fun for both of you. Some owners enjoy the training so much that they go on to compete in a variety of training competitions with their dogs, meeting people and making new friends along the way.

You should be the most interesting thing in your dog's life. So many people take their dog to the local park, let him off the leash to run riot with all the other dogs, then put a leash on him

Below: Family dogs watching while children play in the park on the way home from school used to be a common sight; but thoughtless dog owners and new regulations mean many parks now ban dogs.

again and take him home. As the owner, you should be encouraging your dog to prefer to be with you, using whatever incentives are necessary. While it is nice for your dog to socialize with other dogs, it should not be at the cost of basic control. Free running is great exercise and fun for the dog, but he should only be allowed this if he will respond reliably to you as his owner.

Frequent Recall

So many people make the mistake of only recalling the dog and putting the leash on when they are ready to go home. It does not take a bright dog long to realize this and he may go deaf at the recall request. Sensible owners

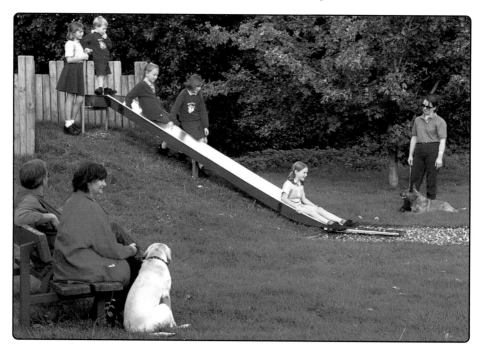

should be frequently recalling their dogs, praising them for coming, and giving a variety of rewards. Sometimes the reward may be a tasty treat, or a game with a special toy, or at other times a pat and cuddle before instructing the dog to "GO AND PLAY" again. It does not do any harm to put the leash back on the dog occasionally, do a few minutes training and then reward your dog by telling him that he may go and play again.

Above: You can reward your dog for a prompt response to returning when called by producing a toy from your pocket and having a short game. Put the toy away while your dog still wants to play.

Keeping Your Dog Under Control

If the dog will not respond off the leash then it should be kept on the leash for its own and others' safety. More and more public areas are making stringent conditions for dog walkers, fencing off sections where dogs are not allowed and expecting that owners will clean up after their dogs. In the few areas where children's playgrounds are not segregated, it is vitally important that dogs be kept under control.

It is the most natural thing in the world to take the dog for a walk and the children to play in the park. Common sense says that it is almost impossible to watch the children and the dog if they are all running around in different directions. Even if the dog is normally well behaved when off the leash, it may be more socially acceptable to keep him on the leash while supervising the children. This can also be an ideal opportunity to practice basic control exercises. Even the friendliest dog can pose a danger to a small child if one or both are over-excited and the child gets knocked over. Owners should always be aware that even the most laid-back dog can react totally out of character if suddenly taken by surprise.

Familiarization Is the Key

If you have a young puppy, you can do much to help shape his character by familiarizing him with normal daily occurrences. So many owners, when they find that they have a problem with their dog wanting to chase joggers or cyclists, go out of their way to avoid meeting the problem. We believe it is much more sensible to confront the issue and teach the dog that his behavior is inappropriate.

Spending the day watching a local marathon, for example, gives plenty of opportunity to show your dog how he should behave, and then you can reward him accordingly. This is far

Above: However playful and friendly this Retriever's intentions may be toward a passing cyclist, the potential for an accident and injury should be obvious. Think ahead of your dog.

more beneficial than a lifetime spent avoiding such problems. If you make sufficient effort, the trigger that caused your dog's bad behavior can be switched to produce good behavior: so your dog now sees a jogger as a signal that if he does not attempt to chase, he will be rewarded.

Start Basic Handling Right Away
Our training courses assume that owners can handle their dogs, and that means more than just putting on a collar and leash. This might sound a very obvious statement, but it never fails to amaze us how many people say "I do not do that because he doesn't like it," meaning they cannot touch their dog unless he chooses to let them.

No one is suggesting that your dog should submit to being mauled by all and sundry, but it is essential that your family is able, at the very least, to administer basic care. They should be able to handle him thoroughly for grooming, bathing when necessary, veterinary examinations, and so on.

Where young puppies are concerned, they may be ticklish and not yet require serious grooming, but they should be accustomed to it at an early stage to prevent problems later. It is much easier to gently but firmly insist with an eight week-old puppy rather than try the same handling with an eight month-old young adult.

A few minutes daily spent brushing his baby coat, checking his ears, teeth, feet, and toenails will pay dividends in the long run. A dog will soon learn to enjoy these one-to-one moments with his owner.

Throughout this book we stress how important it is to praise your dog quietly and calmly – and perhaps you can encourage your dog also by rewarding him with a treat.

Grooming Benefits

It is worthwhile to occasionally trim or at least go through the motions of trimming his nails. Many dogs do not need their nails clipped because the exercise they get keeps them short. However, in old age dogs tend to take less exercise and it is not unusual for their nails to need clipping for comfort. If your dog is not used to this he can get very stressed and unhappy.

If you have just got an older dog or rescue dog, particularly if they are not used to being handled or have unfortunate associations with it, they will need to become accustomed slowly and steadily to the handling.

Do not try and do too much at once; very short sessions ending in a reward, even if you have not groomed his entire coat, can be built up over time. Many dogs particularly dislike having their toenails clipped, so owners often hand this problem over to the vet or dog-groomer. This may be even more stressful for the dog as the vet, or groomer, is obliged to do all four feet in one session. How much kinder if the owner were to take the time to do *one nail* a day, rewarding with praise and a treat so that it is a pleasant experience. It will not be long before all four feet can be done in one session.

Visiting the Vet

Sooner or later all dogs need to visit the vet, even if only for booster vaccinations. During these visits the vet will usually give the dog a general health check. If you have already taken the time to handle, groom, and nail clip your dog, then the visit will be much more pleasant and beneficial for all concerned.

If there are any health concerns

Left and right: Two alternative methods of checking the dog's feet and nails. Both are correct, allowing thorough examination between the pads and around the base of the nails. Dew claws should be checked too.

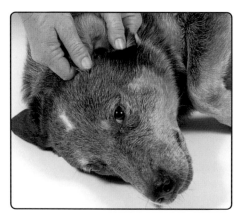

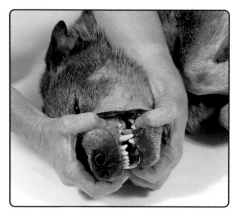

regarding your dog this can have an effect on how, when, and what training he does. If a dog has a medical problem, for example hip dysplasia, where there is a risk of causing your dog pain, then the training approach must be adapted accordingly.

Training to Encourage, Not to Punish

Try to have a positive attitude. If your dog is obviously just about to do something such as chase a cat, or is caught in the act then by all means say "NO," but then try to follow it up immediately with positive commands so that he can be praised. This decisive approach should be used whenever possible as it applies to almost every aspect of the dog's life, from house-

Top: Examining the dog's ears for dirt or foreign bodies should be done regularly, especially if the dog goes swimming – water in the ears will encourage canker.

Above: Your dog should be familiar with having his teeth and mouth checked. Doggy toothbrushes and toothpastes are available, although our dogs have large raw marrow bones that they chew to help keep their teeth clean.

Above: A veterinary examination can be very stressful, but if you and your family have given your dog plenty of gentle handling it will cause less problems. If your dog will not allow you to examine him, what chance has the poor vet?

Below: Strange though it may seem, ignoring your dog totally can be one of the most effective punishments you can use. It may be difficult not to respond to his incessant barking for attention, but by reprimanding him, you are simply heeding his demand.

training onward.

When to Say "NO!"

So many people reprimand their dog long after the event, by which time the dog has forgotten about it and does not understand why he is being told off. For example, if an owner comes back from shopping and finds that his dog has chewed the leg of the antique table it is too late to tell him off. Dragging him over to point out the damage while scolding him will only confuse him. If the dog learns anything from that, it will be that he should be afraid when his owner returns home.

However, if your dog is caught in the act of chewing, a sharp "NO!" should stop him instantly; but then give him something he *can* chew on, his bone or toy, and praise him for chewing that. Whatever your dog may be doing that you do not like, rather than nagging him "NO! NO! NO!," try to channel his behavior toward something that is acceptable so that you can praise him.

Persistent Barking

Another common problem we find where owners inadvertently give the wrong signals to their dogs is with persistent barking. Shouting "NO! BE QUIET!" (or something similar) appears to the dog to be confirming the need for noise. Dogs bark for many different reasons, sometimes to warn the household of possible intruders, perhaps the postman, at other times it is just to seek attention. Most people do want their dog to warn off strangers, but not to excess. If the reason for barking is justified, you should acknowledge your dog's warning but then take charge of the situation. Instruct your dog to "SIT" or "DOWN" quietly by your side, or perhaps command him to go to his bed. This should divert your dog's attention from barking without the need for constant reprimanding. The dog can

Below and opposite: This young Labrador is having a good chew on the wicker chair on which he is standing. When the owner comes in and obviously catches him in the act, the owner is justified in reprimanding with a firm "NO!" and removing him from the chair. The owner recognizes that the youngster has a need to chew on something and offers a more appropriate toy. Treat balls, which can have a tasty morsel placed inside, help to keep the dog interested in the correct chew.

then be praised for responding correctly.

Barking as Attention-seeking

If the dog is barking just to seek attention, then any attention is better than none. Try to look at this from the dog's point of view: he is barking to seek attention; so what happens? You go to your dog, usually to yell at him, but the dog thinks he has "won," as he has got the attention he wanted. This has reinforced his impression that you will come when called.

The best possible way to deal with this type of barking is to ignore it completely. Initially this may be difficult, but if the dog gets no response he will usually cease making a noise. As soon as he is quiet then you can reward him. If the dog is especially persistent then, for the sake of the neighbors, it may be necessary to interrupt his behavior. Ideally, this should be something unexpected which

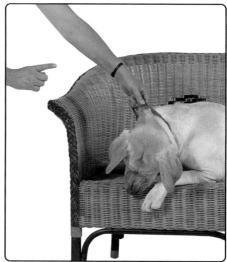

makes him pause for breath, such as suddenly banging a metal tray. The quiet pause can then be praised and the dog's attention focused elsewhere.

Dogs Are Not Humans

Another common problem we come across in our training sessions is that owners insist on treating their dogs as little people and not as dogs. Endowing a dog with human characteristics often causes unnecessary problems.

Frustrated owners will accuse their dog of bearing a grudge, or complain that he has misbehaved in class to spite them (for yelling at their dog earlier). This is simply not the case, and when the situation has been reviewed and seen from the dog's point of view, this usually eases the tension and allows training to progress to resolve the conflict. Of course we all cuddle our dogs and chat to them, hopefully showing them affection which they enjoy. But remember, it is the pleasant tones and obvious attention, rather than the explicit meaning of the words, which makes it seem that they understand everything you say.

As a footnote, we would also add that we do not profess to know all the answers on understanding dogs, and even after having helped train thousands of dogs of all breeds, we never stop learning.

How Dogs Learn

Dogs learn by trial and reward. If they do something by accident or design and get a pleasant result, then they are more likely to repeat the behavior. Alternatively, if there is no reward at all or they are scolded, they are less likely to repeat it. You should be creating situations which will give your dog plenty of opportunity for rewarding experiences.

You need to find out what motivates your dog, what he likes and what will get him to respond to your training best. You need to show him that responding well to your training brings rewards. Thankfully, puppies and most dogs are willing to please, and this can be cultivated as they learn to look to you for guidance.

Whether your dog is an extrovert, or shy and reserved, the principle of trial and reward is the same. The extrovert will probably experience more learning situations as he rushes in head-first, but will recover quickly from any setbacks. The shy dog will be more cautious in his approach and will usually take longer to recover. The sensible owner will try and introduce his dog to as many non-threatening situations as possible to widen the dog's horizons and build his confidence.

Learning Curve
As instructors, one of the most rewarding aspects of taking training classes is seeing introverted dogs blossom into much happier characters with positive handling. This learning curve is not dependent on any formal training. The puppy which falls in the water bowl and does not like the experience will tend to be more careful next time, whereas the puppy who found it great fun splashing around in the water will be permanently wet.

We can harness this learning by using trial and reward in our approach to training. The key is to reward favorably the behavior that you want, as it is then likely to be repeated. This does not mean spoiling him with endless unearned treats and never yelling at him. What it does mean is using a combination of food treats, plenty of affection when you want to give it, and dedicated time for play.

Seeking a Balance
You need to ignore or chastise any behavior from your dog which is not acceptable. Most children, if asked, would like an endless supply of sweets; unlimited television, video, and computer games; and going to bed when they liked. But sensible parents realize that this would be detrimental in the long term and so try to steer a course between praise for good behavior and ignoring any attention-seeking.

Left: All puppies should be handled gently and frequently. They should be accustomed to being restrained quietly, but firmly, so that if it should be necessary for them to have veterinary treatment for example, they will not find this unduly stressful.

The Art of Reprimanding

A reward or chastisement needs to be tailored to the individual dog – and at the appropriate time (for example immediately when the behavior occurs). A common occurrence is the dog which does not return when called. Eventually the dog does return only to be greeted with a severe scolding. The owner is scolding the dog for not coming back when called, but in the dog's mind he is being scolded *for* coming back. Dogs do not generally think or reason like humans (contrary to popular belief); they associate being reprimanded with what they are doing *now*, not with what they did *earlier*. Therefore, even the dog who is totally innocent can be made to appear "guilty" by the owner's body language and harsh voice.

Frustrating though it may be, you should be praising him for returning, and if there is an art to dog training it is in being able to say, "Good Dog, you little ********!" in a sincerely happy tone with a smile on your face.

Above: Cute and cuddly he may look, but do not be fooled. In a few months this will be an active dog of a working breed. Firm and fair handling together with love and affection will guide him in the right direction.

Dogs Are Individuals

Remember that all dogs are different. Concentration span can vary within breeds as well as with age. Young puppies tire more quickly, both mentally and physically, than older pups or adult dogs. Even within litters there will be variation just as there is with brothers and sisters in the same human family. The owner's ability and experience will also have an effect.

Some puppies may appear to be very bright and catch on quickly, others will appear much slower and require more repetitions of training exercises. Do not despair if you appear to have one of the latter. Experience has shown us that the apparently fast learner can also forget just as quickly – while the apparently slow dog may take longer but be just as reliable in the end.

Whatever the breed of dog, it is natural especially for a young puppy or adolescent to see what it can get away with in terms of behavior. This needs keeping a check on so that it does not get out of hand, but praising for his good behavior is more beneficial.

Breed Characteristics

Remember that while all breeds are capable of learning training exercises, it is wise to consider the breed characteristics before you start. For example, small breeds mature more quickly both physically and mentally than large breeds. Scent hounds were bred to follow their noses – ask any Beagle or Basset Hound owner how deaf their dogs can go when they pick up an interesting scent – while Terriers usually have strong characters and are very tenacious. All breeds were developed with a purpose in mind.

The owner, or potential owner, would be wise to acquaint themselves with the origins of their chosen pet as this may affect their approach to training and expectations. These days most planned breeding is to produce pets and show dogs. Very few dogs have the opportunity to fulfill their original function, but the instincts will still be there. Time spent researching books, magazines, breed clubs, and talking to owners who already have the same breed will pay dividends.

Body Language

Although dogs can be very vocal animals, their main method of communication is by non-verbal signals, or what we call body language. Dogs use their bodies in many different ways to communicate to each other and to us. Understanding their body language, as well as our own and what that means to our dogs, is therefore crucial.

The endless stream of excellent wildlife programs on television has probably given the majority of the general public an insight into animal communication. With dogs, many of their behavioral traits have been well illustrated in programs about wolves. Although some of these signals have been toned down in the domestic dog, many are recognizably the same.

Picking Up Signals

Dogs are much more aware of body language than their owners are: one only has to see an older experienced dog appear to anticipate his owner's instructions. In fact, what has usually happened is that the dog has recognized the body language and knows what instructions are coming. Changes in attitude are frequently picked up by the dog regardless of the owner's intentions. Many owners comment to us that their dogs know when they are happy or sad.

Body language to the dog is your posture and stance, which he interprets rightly or wrongly. The dog who appears "guilty" when the owner arrives home to find his slippers destroyed would appear just as "guilty" if the owner came storming in annoyed at being stuck in a traffic jam. In the first instance the owner would interpret the dog's lowered posture, wagging tail, and fawning behavior as "knowing he was guilty." In the second case, the same behavior on the part of the dog would probably be interpreted by the owner as sympathy for his bad day. If only owners were as observant as their dogs.

Above: Puppies solicit food from their mothers and other adults by licking at their mouths so food is regurgitated. Such behavior clearly indicates to this mature dog (right) that the younger dog is only a baby and poses no threat.

Reaction Dictates Response

The subtle differences in posture and behavior, which indicate how your dog is feeling, are frequently missed altogether or misread. For example, a puppy with his hackles up from his ears to the base of his tail is usually frightened rather than aggressive. The owner's reaction therefore often dictates the dog's response.

Dogs rarely "suddenly" bite. Usually there will have been many warning signs, such as low growls if the dog has been moved off the settee, or a stiff, momentarily frozen stance over the food bowl as the owner comes near, or increasing possessiveness of toys. These signs, together with a reluctance to do as requested unless it suits him, should be heeded.

Below: The larger dog exudes confidence from his slowly wagging tail to his arched neck giving every indication that he is in charge. The younger female dog has responded to the larger dog's head over her shoulders by lying down.

Learning from Their Mothers

There are many excellent books on inherited and learned behavior in dogs. Our book is about training rather than behavior, but you should realize that both types of behavior occur and can be channelled to your advantage.

Dogs start to develop their understanding of canine body language while still with their mother and the rest of the litter. The rough play of puppies teaches them how to behave with each other. This might seem to be stating the obvious, but it is through this play that a dog learns to communicate with his own kind.

This can be one of the reasons why puppies who have been taken from the nest too early, or are "only" pups, develop problems. They have missed the opportunity to interact with their peer group and thus can lack the skills to communicate with other dogs. A bitch who is a good mother can help

alleviate this as she feeds, cares for, and plays with her offspring.

If you are concerned that your dog will not like you if you are firm, then watch a bitch disciplining her boisterous pups. When one of them has done something which she considers to be wrong – perhaps nipped her too hard – she bowls the offender over, her upright stance and body posture giving every impression that she is about to kill him. The sensible puppy is the picture of submission – on his side or back, legs in the air, ears back, avoiding eye-contact, tail probably between his legs, and possibly even urinating as well.

As time goes on the puppy learns to read the signals so that all the bitch needs to do is give a look and the puppy will understand completely. A particularly pushy puppy may keep

testing to see what he can get away with, and require more lessons from his mother before he will comply. Once he has left his mother, the puppy needs to continue interacting with other dogs if he is to maintain these social skills.

Dogs try and apply these learned interpretations to their dealings with people and their new family. They frequently pick up the body language before they associate it with the verbal command. Hopefully any previous owners have smiled and handled them in a kind and pleasant manner, making calm and friendly sounds at the same time. Thus the puppy learns that bared teeth in a smiling human is a sign of friendship not aggression. In some cases dogs even learn to mimic this and will "smile" at you.

Getting On Your Dog's Level

When meeting a puppy, most people tend to automatically crouch down to enable them to have hands-on contact. This also has the effect of making them appear to the puppy, smaller and less threatening. It is worth remembering

Left: The younger female dog has submitted totally, rolling over in front of the more mature dog, ears back accepting his position. Her tail is tucked but wagging to show that she wants to be friendly and is not looking for an argument.

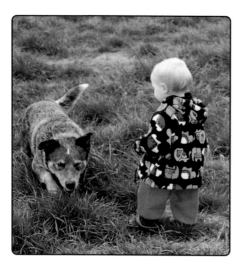

Above: Small children can be easily knocked over and hurt by an exuberant dog whatever the size. Children and dogs should never be left unsupervised. What starts as a game can so easily end in tears.

Do not under any circumstances raise your voice or try to grab the puppy. Keep your body posture low and avoid sudden movements; speak in a soft, gentle encouraging voice. The puppy should then realize that you are pleased with him and be confident to come the rest of the way.

Dealing with a Cheeky Puppy

The other scenario is the cheeky, confident puppy who comes flying back when called only to stop a few feet in front of you. His body language says it all: tail wagging, head cocked to one side, and whites of his eyes showing. He will also often drop into a "play bow" with his front end down and his tail in the air. It is quite evident that he is saying "Chase me!"

If you are silly enough to take a step toward him, he will either back off a few paces or be off with his ears back and tail between his legs doing circuits around you in great glee before he returns to start the game again. Resist the urge to launch yourself at him; you might succeed the first time you try but the puppy will learn to be faster next time. The more you flail your arms about and shout, the more fun the puppy believes you are having. Try to keep calm, and if you have a toy or treat, produce it and try to lure him in. Do not grab him but make sure that you do not relinquish the toy or treat until you have hold of his collar.

Some puppies still avoid contact in favor of a hoped-for game. Try to ignore

this if you are some distance from your youngster when you call him. The raised voice, intended to carry the sound to the dog, together with the upright posture can appear very intimidating. If your dog appears hesitant as it looks toward you, crouch down and the dog will come running.

What happens next depends on your actions and the temperament of your puppy. Hopefully, he will leap delightedly into your outstretched arms now that he has become confident of his welcome reception.

On the other hand, if his hesitancy was due to him being very timid, he may well come to within a few feet of you and then stop again, still unsure of your response.

such behavior and walk away avoiding eye contact. Usually your disinterested posture will make him come chasing after you to see why you do not want to play anymore. That is the time to crouch down again and encourage him in, maybe with the toy or treat.

Although this is considered chiefly to be puppy-related behavior, such goings-on are frequently seen in older dogs and should be dealt with in the same manner.

Children and Dogs

Many of the problems between children and dogs develop because neither understand the body language of the other. Young children get over-excited, move rapidly and unexpectedly and scream in high pitched tones. Dogs often interpret these as invitations to play when in fact the child may be fearful. Similarly, a dog's attempts to play and be friends can be seen by the child as an attack. Whatever the size of the dog, he will usually try and lick at the child's face as he would another dog (a small dog may have to jump up), and such actions can lead to increasing the child's fear. An exciting game of chase nearly always ends with the child being knocked over, and the dog then believes that the child's howls of distress are an indication of how much fun he is having and jumps on top of him, thus making matters worse. So both dog and child need to be supervised to prevent misunderstandings, and even children who are not frightened and enjoy playing with dogs need to be watched.

Left: This dog realizes there is something wrong with his owner and is concerned because he does not understand her distress and offers a beseeching paw for her attention.

CHAPTER TWO HOW AND WHEN DO I START?

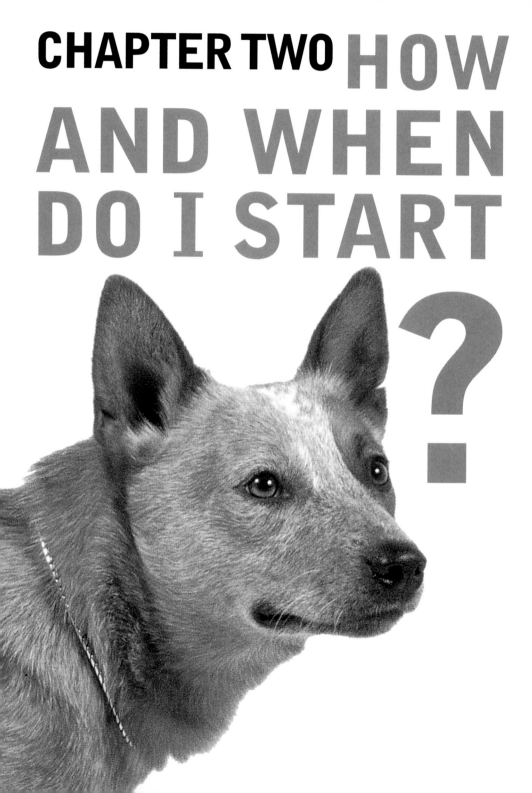

Training Is Timeless

If you have just got a puppy, you should start by teaching him his name, then how to be clean in the house, and also the difference between good and bad. Avoid being negative – some puppies end up thinking their name is "NO." Instead, take a positive attitude as outlined in *Chapter One*, as this can make your dog's introduction to his new home much easier.

Acclimatizing Your Puppy

Before beginning any formal training, try to cultivate habits which will stand you both in good stead for the future. The puppy's inclination is to be with someone, so make use of this by calling his name, commanding "COME" and praising as he does. Patting, a treat, and a game will build up pleasant associations in his mind with the recall at home.

On their first outings to the park, most people want to keep their puppy on the leash in case they lose their dog. If the area is secure it is much more sensible to let the puppy off the leash and encourage him to follow. At a young age the puppy is generally looking for leadership and is afraid of losing you, so he will keep check of where you are. Any hesitancy to come when called can usually be rectified by crouching down and offering encouragement, or moving as if to run away. The puppy must be praised and rewarded for coming to make it worth his while. An adolescent dog who has never been let off the leash might be much harder to recall on his first taste of freedom.

Formal Training Time

Young puppies have a very short concentration span and tire easily, therefore they should not really attend a formal training class until they are older. However, puppy playgroups are becoming more common and can be great fun as well as enormously beneficial for the pups.

Older pups of eighteen weeks or so (depending on the individual and breed) are better able to cope with training sessions. Strong-willed puppies especially may be needing firmer discipline and may be ready for formal training sessions. Bear in mind that however well-behaved the puppy, it is not unusual for him to go through a "teenage rebellious" stage. Nevertheless, sensibly handled puppies will mature into happy and well-adjusted characters.

The Case for More Training

Contrary to the well-known saying, older dogs can be taught new tricks. You may decide, for whatever reason, that your dog needs more training. Perhaps circumstances have changed, for example a new baby in the family, and previously tolerated behavior becomes unacceptable. It can be quite a shock to the dog to have the rules altered. If the changes are to be major, for example restricting his freedom of the house, they may be easier to implement if they occur following other alterations to his routine. If he has been in kennels or you have just move, this can be an ideal opportunity to set up a new regime.

Rescued Dogs

Rescued dogs of any age are usually of an unknown background and may have experienced some degree of trauma. This can mean that instead of starting with a clean sheet one may have to cope with unacceptable behaviors already established. An even greater degree of patience, understanding, and consistency may be required on your part.

While it is nice to allow the dog time to settle in his new home, it is advisable to adhere to clear rules from the beginning. A regular routine should help him settle more quickly. Some thought may need to be given to how he is handled and approached. It may be easy to insist with an eight week old puppy, but it would be foolhardy to try and insist with a large, adult dog. Circumnavigating the issue in the early stages may help break the bad habit. For example, if he stakes a claim to your sofa or double bed and refuses to budge without an argument, it may be more sensible not to allow him access in the future.

As he settles in and you begin to understand each other, he should accept that when you say "MOVE" you mean it. It is worth pointing out that most rescued dogs follow a normal pattern regarding settling in to their new home. The first week or two they are usually on their best behavior, then

Above: A rescued dog's appearance is not necessarily a guide to his temperament – even small dogs can be quite ferocious!

Above: They may look very similar in coloring and size, but each puppy will have its own unique character. Even if two apparently identical puppies go to the same home, they will still develop as individual personalities in their own right, just as children do in the same family.

they test the water and show their true colors. If this can be worked through, they settle down secure in their new home.

A Safe Refuge for Your Dog

Whatever the age of dog being introduced to your home, a safe space that can be his "sanctuary" is essential. It may be that the utility room or a space in the kitchen will suffice, but it is amazing what damage can be caused by canine teeth and claws.

Crate: The arrival on the scene of collapsible dog crates or indoor cages was frowned upon by many people in the dog world who did not understand their use. They were never intended to

be a "cage" that the dog lived in permanently or as a punishment. But if used correctly, they are a versatile training aid helping protect the dog from possible danger, such as electric cables, or from the children, as well as protecting the house and contents from demolition. They are also helpful during house training. Most designs will fold flat and can be moved easily and erected in the car or in a hotel or friend's house when required.

Bed: Introduced in a considerate way, most dogs will quickly come to view their crate as a happy, safe den. Whenever the dog is put in the crate, giving him a small treat and telling him "Bed," will make it a pleasant experience. Our older dogs, who have not needed to be crated for many years, will joyfully take up residence if the crate is erected, wagging their tails waiting for a treat.

The crate should be large enough for the dog to stand up and turn around in comfortably. It is advisable if buying a

Above: Folding crates are a very versatile tool in dog training, as well as keeping the dog, or puppy, safe and secure. While to us it may look like a cage, correctly introduced it soon becomes his den.

crate for your new puppy to get the size which will accommodate him as an adult if necessary. This will mean that as a puppy there will be plenty of room for a comfortable bed with a chew toy and room for newspaper in case he has an accident.

And So to Bed...

Do resist buying an expensive, attractive bed for a puppy as he will probably have great fun chewing it to pieces. Cardboard boxes come in a range of sizes and it is not nearly so upsetting or expensive when you find them in bits! Sufficient space for

newspaper is particularly important for nights. Most puppies, if put to bed very late and taken out very early, quickly learn to be clean overnight. Ideally, during the day, the dog will only be shut in for short periods of time when it is not practical to supervise him properly.

House Training...

Young puppies need to relieve themselves frequently – on waking up after a short nap, after eating, and often during play. It is pointless with a very young puppy to put him outside, shut the door in his face and expect him to go to the toilet. The pup will usually just sit looking up to the door, waiting for the owner to come out and play as well.

Time spent in the first few days going outside with the puppy, and praising him while he performs, will ensure rapid house training. In the early days and weeks it is unrealistic to expect your puppy to "ask" to go outside. It is really up to the owner to realize "that it is probably time" and take the puppy outside. While praising the dog as he performs, use a word or phrase like "HURRY UP" or "BE CLEAN." The puppy will soon make the association between the word and his action. This can be extremely useful later on if away from home or if pushed for time.

His Den, Not the Children's

As the puppy matures or the rescued dog settles in and can be trusted loose in the house, the crate can be dispensed with and replaced by a comfortable dog bed. If he has made happy associations with his bed in the crate then the command "BED" should still send him to his place, where he can be praised and rewarded. Never send the dog to bed as a punishment or he will resent going there. It should be a positive, pleasant experience before he gets into trouble. As we have already said, it should not take long for the dog to view his crate or bed as a safe den. While he should not be allowed to become possessive over them, it is essential that children in particular are taught that even the dog has a right to some peace and quiet.

Right: The dog who understands the command "BED" can be kept out from underfoot where he may get into mischief. For example, the dog cannot beg at the dinner table if he is lying quietly in his bed. It should be made clear to him when you have finished dinner that he may move.

Equipment and Training Aids

Training aids are anything that will help you to train your dog. Your hands and voice, food treats, leash, collar, clicker, and toys are all tools which can be used. Use "tools" that will enable you and your dog to succeed in a pleasant and enjoyable way for both of you. The essential tool, however, is you the trainer working one-to-one with your dog.

The methods explained in this book are the ones that we use and teach on our courses, and which we have found work well for the majority of dogs.

We recommend that you start teaching your dog on a one-to-one basis because dog training is a bit like learning a foreign language. Different tones of voice, timing, and accents make it harder for the dog to understand what is required. Once he has started to understand then others can work with him using the same commands.

In dog training a dog is customarily worked on the owner's left-hand side and for the purposes of this book it is assumed that is where your dog will be.

Right: You should be appropriately dressed. Comfortable clothing should be worn, including flat shoes. It is important that you are not worrying about soiling your clothes with dirty paws or jewellery getting caught up in your dog's teeth or feet.

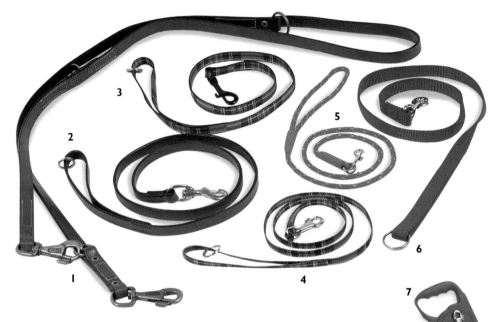

Above: A 6ft (2m) double-clipped leather training leash (1) can be useful, but a good 3–4ft (1m) leather leash is ideal for training (2). Nylon (3,4), rope (5), or canvas (6) are also suitable. A ring in the handle will enable the leash to be kept short with ease for close work by clipping the trigger hook onto the ring before attaching to the collar.

A split ring, such as a key-ring, can be fitted if the leash does not already have one. Under certain circumstances, extending leashes (7), head collars, and harnesses can also all be useful.

Voice

Your voice is your link to your dog. It commands, praises, or scolds. When you begin training, make your commands firmly but nicely. You do not have to shout at your dog to make him understand. When you say your dog's name say it nicely, when you praise him be enthusiastic, when you scold more or less growl at him.

Praise

Praising your dog is the most important part of training. It is the best way to let him know he has done well and you are pleased with him. Praise warmly and pat him as his primary reward. The praise should be geared toward the individual dog's temperament. If he is very excitable then it should be calm praise, but if he is a couch potato then it should be more dynamic.

Hands

Your hands show the dog what to do: they will teach, praise, and correct him. Your dog should enjoy the physical contact and feel trust in your hands.

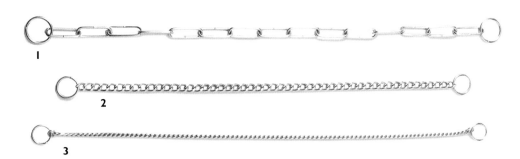

Above: Choke chains come in a variety of weights, lengths, and shapes of link, but they all do the same job: (1) a long link, (2) a medium-weight flat link, (3) a fine flat link.

Patience, Firmness, and Kindness

These are virtues in training that you need to employ. To train your dog successfully, remember to employ these three essentials in equal amounts. Keep in mind also that a well-trained dog is not an instant commodity.

Commands

This does not mean screaming instructions at your dog nor being a bully; it does mean, however, being firm and fair. Dogs like to know the rules. Remember, a command is an instruction not a request, and is not optional.

Giving Commands

Commands must be given clearly and you must avoid confusion. Say "SIT" not "SIT DOWN;" this is two commands at once and will confuse a trained dog. "SIT" is sit and "DOWN" means "lie flat on the floor." "OFF," for example, means "do not jump up" or "get off the sofa."

Listen to the rest of the family, if they all tend to say "SIT DOWN" and "DOWN" meaning "Do not jump up," then it may be easier to teach everyone a new command. You could make "FLAT" mean "Lie down on the ground." Ultimately, it does not really matter what the commands are so long as they are used consistently. It is also the tone not the volume which is important.

It is just as important to let the dog know when an exercise has been completed. Use a "release" word or phrase such as "That will do" or That's it," not "Good dog," or he may move whenever you try to praise him. "Good Dog" means "Keep doing what you are doing, it is right;" it does not mean "You are finished and it's okay to run around."

Time Out

If you are having a bad day and everything seems to be going wrong or you're coming down with flu, then leave the training alone. The occasional day missed will not hurt, but if you find you are missing every other day then you cannot expect to progress. Similarly, do not expect the dog's co-operation and enjoyment if he has a full tummy after dinner, is overly tired, needs to relieve himself, or is feeling off.

Mistakes Become Habits

We have a saying in our training sessions that goes "Once is a mistake, twice is a habit." If you allow your dog to repeat a mistake continually on an exercise, it will become a habit. When we teach our training classes we emphasise the need to be precise and to expect and obtain a prompt response from the dog.

We liken it to learning to drive; you are expected to sit up very straight in a car, hold the hands just so on the steering wheel, concentrate, look in the mirrors before indicating, manoeuvring, and so on.

Above: There is a right and a wrong way to put on a chain. This is the correct way: when the dog is at the owner's left side, put the collar over the dog's head, so that the chain goes from the leash over the back of the dog's neck and returns underneath. When fitted this way, the chain can tighten and fall loose.

Above: The choke chain should be long enough to slide comfortably over the dog's head, but when pulled tight should have only 2–4in (5–10cm) of chain up to the end of the leash.

Above: If you fit a choke chain upside down by mistake, the chain will tighten but cannot then be slackened on the dog's neck. You must remove the chain and put it back on the correct way.

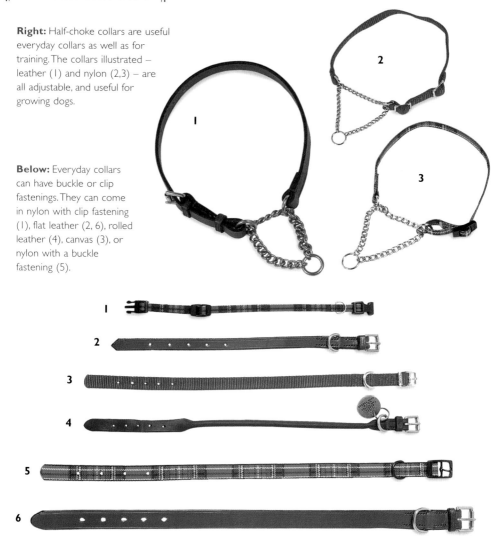

Right: Half-choke collars are useful everyday collars as well as for training. The collars illustrated – leather (1) and nylon (2,3) – are all adjustable, and useful for growing dogs.

Below: Everyday collars can have buckle or clip fastenings. They can come in nylon with clip fastening (1), flat leather (2, 6), rolled leather (4), canvas (3), or nylon with a buckle fastening (5).

After passing the driving test (aside from relief) you tend to get more "relaxed" about driving – but never compromising on being a safe and competent driver. We apply the same attitude to our training, if you allow sloppy responses in the early stages then you cannot expect a quick and accurate response at a later stage. Start as you mean to go on: give one command, help your dog give the correct response, then praise him. Do not keep repeating the command. Always be ready to help the dog respond instantly so that praise can be given and a good habit formed. At all times in training you must show, teach, and reward.

Above: For a correct half-choke collar fit, when the loose ring on the chain is pulled tight, the two ends of the neck strap should be about an inch apart on the dog's neck.

Above: In this half-choke collar position the two ends are too close together.

Collars

Baby puppies should have a closely fitting buckled or clipped collar. These should be tight enough to only allow two fingers to be squeezed underneath them; otherwise, the dog will be able to slide free. As they get older, age, size, and temperament will have a bearing on which collar is most appropriate. Some placid dogs may always wear a correctly-fitted buckle-type collar. More boisterous dogs may move on to a half-choke, which gives a greater degree of control but is less demanding than a check chain.

We mostly use a half-choke or a choke chain. Should your dog need a choke chain, it should be the size he needs now, not the one he is expected to grow into. Choke chains should never be left on an unattended dog or used as an everyday collar. They should only be used for training purposes.

Using a Leash

When a leash is attached to a half-choke or a choke chain, the collar must be kept loose around the dog's neck. Apart from being cruel, your dog cannot learn if the collar is tight around his neck all the time. Clips on the end of the leash vary in style; we prefer the bolt type trigger hook. A chain leash will chafe your hands while an all-in-one collar and leash is of limited use for teaching basic obedience, as there is no collar to hold onto when the leash is removed. The leash should be comfortable for you to work with and an appropriate weight for your dog's size.

CHAPTER THREE
TRAINING METHODS

Rewarding Your Dog

In theory there are many different methods of dog training; in practice there is a great deal of overlap between most of them. For example, praise can be used with food or toys, and toys can be used instead of food with a clicker. Ultimately, the object of the exercise is to reward your dog in a manner suitable to him.

What is praise? For many dogs a quiet word and pat from their owner makes them squirm with delight; but others would sell their souls for a tasty treat. One thing is certain: if the method you use works, do not try and change it.

Timing Is the Trick

If there is a trick to dog training, whatever the method, we believe that it is in the timing of the correction and praise. The correction, if required, needs to be applied at the precise moment that the mistake occurs. This should be sufficient to deter your dog, and can then be followed promptly by praise with the emphasis on praise. Training should be fun for you and the dog, and should not be looked upon as a chore that needs to be done.

Praising Your Dog

Everyone likes to be praised for a job well done and dogs are no exception. Though they do not understand the exact meaning of the words, dogs very easily understand the tone of them. Therefore, the praise must sound genuine

Right: A quiet moment with dog and owner enjoying physical contact and relaxing in between exercises. You should always take time out just to appreciate contact and companionship with your dog.

even though your patience may have worn a bit thin. Hearing the pleasure and enthusiasm in your voice is one of the prime motivators for your dog.

Getting the Right Pitch
As already mentioned, your voice and hands are a natural link to your dog. You do not have to make a conscious effort to remember to pick them up and take them with you. The gentle tone of your voice can calm a boisterous dog or give confidence and reassurance to a timid dog. It can also indicate to your dog that he has done something wrong.

Women usually have an advantage in this respect when praising as they tend to have a greater range of pitch. However, they can lack the lower tone for reprimand. Men have the opposite problem and lack the higher pitch for praise. Again, we should stress that we are talking about tone not volume. A dog's hearing is more acute than ours; therefore, if he is only a leash's length away, you do not need to shout at him. What are you going to do if he is some 200yd (180m) away? Keeping your voice down also encourages him to pay attention to you, especially if you follow up with an action, whether that be patting, playing, or training. You should be able to play with your dog without the need for a toy. Some dogs like to play "catch my toes," others enjoy a more physical game of "push and shove." You should be able to start and stop games when you chose, and certainly not leave it up to the dog to dictate when these will be played.

Respect
Owners who have a good relationship with their dog usually find that their dog respects them and delights in the praise and attention whenever it is offered. The opposite to this is the dog who has little or no respect for a doting owner who smothers his dog with verbal and physical praise which he has done nothing to deserve. This type of dog demands attention when he wants it, and walks away from it when he has had enough.

This is especially obvious when he is outdoors in a park and sees everything else as more interesting than his owner. A dog should always find it more rewarding to be interacting with his owner, and taking pleasure in being part of the "pack."

Above: These dogs are having a great game in the garden together, but if they have any respect for their owner, they will abandon it in favour of playing with the owner.

Right: This puppy is learning that his owner is in charge; the puppy is lying on his back with his feet in the air in a submissive position having his tummy tickled. All puppies should learn to accept having to adopt this position. Another benefit it that medical evidence has shown that stroking your dog can lower your blood pressure.

All of us like to enjoy the company of our dogs and the pleasure in stroking and talking to them should be mutual. However, this is vastly different to the owner who babbles incessantly morning, noon, and night so the dog no longer listens. This type of dog may work better for food, toys, or a clicker.

Every Step of the Way

Another advantage of the praise method is that it is very easy to reward each small step in the right direction. A gentle pat and word of praise, given at the right time for each part of an exercise, soon leashs to a dog being confident in its understanding of the whole exercise.

As we have stressed before, "Good Dog" should signify to the dog that it is doing the right thing and should continue, not that it is being released to play. You should have a clear word or phrase which will make it plain to the dog that he has finished the exercise and may move. It does not matter what words or phrase you use – "That will do," "That's it," "Okay," or whatever comes most easily to mind is fine – so long as you try to be consistent.

Below: This young Labrador's body posture shows his delight as the owner instigates a game with him. No toys or treats are being used, just the mutual pleasure in contact with each other.

Ignore Early Mistakes

While your dog is learning, try to ignore any mistakes he makes. Instead, help him to succeed so that you can praise him. If the mistake is one of anticipation in his enthusiasm to try and please, then do not get cross as you may put him off completely. Gently rectify the mistake and carry on the training.

However, if he is deliberately being defiant, a sharp verbal rebuke is generally all that is required. You should then continue the exercise, helping him so that praise can be given.

Try to recognize the difference between a dog that is unsure of what is required and one that is being deliberately naughty. If your dog has responded correctly once or twice, this does not mean that he understands the command. Reprimanding the unsure dog causes confusion in his mind and he may lose trust in you.

Clicker

The clicker is a tool which can help you communicate with your dog. It does not have to be used for the rest of the dog's life. Once your dog understands what is required of him and the behavior has been given a name – "SIT," "DOWN," and so on – then the clicker can be dispensed with, unless needed to teach something new.

The basic principle is that the noise, the "click," indicates to the dog that he has done something right. The noise is followed by a reward, usually food or a toy. One of the advantages to clicker training is that the food does not have to be given at the same moment as the click. In fact, it should not be given immediately. This means that the dog can be told, while at a distance from you, that he has done something correctly, and he can then return for the reward. Properly taught, the dog will learn that he can earn rewards and he will look for ways to do so.

This is enormously beneficial with dog owners who have dogs that pay them little heed. In order to attract the dog's attention, the owner talks to and fusses over the dog excessively, so much so in fact that the words and patting cease to have any great value to the dog.

A dog must learn to associate the click with the reward, and for simplicity, we shall discuss this using food (*see page 46*).

Below: The clicker is a small plastic device with a metal strip inside which when pressed and released makes a clicking noise – hence the name. Clicker training has been around for many years. It has its roots in dolphin training in the United States from where it has evolved.

Below: When starting clicker training, you should keep quiet and concentrate on watching the dog so that the click will be given at the right moment. This tends to improve your sense of timing as well as encouraging your dog to look at you as he is not being given a continuous verbal signal.

Using a Clicker with Treats

The treats should be tiny, so that your dog can have lots of them without filling up, and they should be tasty. Try cheese, sausage, or liver. Other dogs are happy to work for some of their complete dried food, especially if it is just before meal time. Remember to watch his weight and adjust his meals if necessary to allow for many treats. The treats should be kept on the side or in a pocket and not held in the hand as a continual lure.

Start with a click, then give your dog a treat, and repeat this five or six times. Do this in different places as you do not want your dog to think this only happens in one spot. The next time you click, wait to see if your dog actively looks for a treat. If he does, then he has made the connection and you can move on.

Using the click indicates the end of your dog's action, so do not use a repeated "click, click, click" to try and get the dog to continue doing something such as "STAY."

If you are expecting your dog to complete an exercise that is made up of many parts, then each bit will need to be taught, and clicked, as separate exercises first. Then they can be strung together and clicked once at the end of the "string." When teaching heelwork, for example, you may expect your dog to sit at heel, look at you, step off with you, keep at heel, sit when you stop, and look up at you before being released. You would therefore need to teach your dog each step at a time.

Right: Another training aid which can been used with clicker training is the "target stick" (a lightweight pole). This effectively works as an extension of the owner's arm. Some clicker trainers start by teaching the dog to "target" their hand or finger. In other words, whenever the dog touches the hand with his nose he gets a click and treat.

Catching Attention with a Clicker

Either wait for your dog to assume a position and then click and give a treat, or lure him with a treat in your hand for the first time or two. If your dog is standing or moving around and you decide to start with a sit, then a treat held above his head and moved slightly back will usually get the desired response from him.

When your dog sits, you should not be giving any verbal signals, but you should click once and then toss the treat so that your dog moves out of the sit. If you reward him in the sit, he may decide not to move and just wait for more. Having moved, your dog will probably come sniffing around looking for more treats. Wait to see if your dog shows any signs of sitting.

If not, he may need to be lured to help him make the connection between his action and the click and reward. Most dogs catch on very quickly and will come back and sit, tail wagging. The treat should be tossed in different directions and you should move around as well, so the response is going to be to you and not to the location.

Once your dog is offering to sit promptly after each treat, then the time is right to wait for a stand, down, or other position. Initially, he will be confused because now, if he comes and offers to sit, you will ignore him. He will probably try it a few times and may look very puzzled. If he does not attempt to offer a stand or a down then it may be necessary to lure him into one. In a few short sessions, your dog will have realized that he can "earn" treats and will try and work out what you require him to do. Once that happens, and if you are imaginative, the possibilities are endless.

Left: The target can be transferred to the end of the "target stick," the dog will then follow the end of the pole and can be induced to touch almost anything or to turn in circles, figures of eight and so on.

Food and Toys

You can use food or toys as bonus rewards for your dog, but keep it in conjunction with verbal praise. Although many people would like to think that using toys or food treats are totally independent training methods, in reality there are many similarities. Dogs are motivated by many different things and the key to success is finding the one or ones to suit your dog. As with children who can get bored with being given the same sweet all the time, so a variety is much more interesting to them.

Bite-size Morsels

Food treats should be very small and tasty so they will be eaten quickly. Small means bite-size morsels which can almost be swallowed whole. Do not waste time giving large-sized treats, which more fussy dogs will take ages to finish or greedy dogs will become obsessed about looking for crumbs on the ground. The ideal is small cubes of cheese or diced sausages.

Another treat loved by many dogs is cat biscuits, especially if they think they have stolen them from the cat. They are a handy size for most breeds, and can be carried loose in the pocket without too much mess and are readily

Right: This young crossbred Terrier still has his milk teeth. Care must be taken not to be overly rough while playing with the rope. Although it is normal for the milk teeth to fall out, you do not want him to lose them too soon. If they are pulled out prematurely, it may be very painful and damage his gums.

Left: As is plainly obvious, this adult German Shepherd Dog is relishing this vigorous tug of war game with his owner. They are using a large, hard ball on a rope which the Shepherd will release on command. The owner can then throw the ball, which the dog will be enthusiastic to retrieve so the game can continue.

available. If you are using lots of food treats, make sure to watch your dog's weight. It is quite surprising how quickly small treats can add up in terms of calories (as unfortunately many trainers know).

Safe and Handy Toys

Toys are almost anything which your dog likes to play with, provided they are safe and handy to use. The age and breed of your dog will also have a bearing on the preferred toy. Puppies who still have milk teeth are generally better off with a soft toy, as a hard one can hurt their gums and knock their teeth out. When the puppy is teething it is possible that his mouth will be

very sore and he may not want to play with any type of toy. Once their adult teeth are established, harder toys are often appreciated. It should be worth noting that many people assume that once the adult teeth are showing the puppy will stop chewing. This is not necessarily so. While the adult teeth bed down in the gums sometimes the dog that has never chewed before will go through a "chewing phase." If appropriate toys are supplied, this phase will wear off.

Training toys should be "special" and not left lying around for your dog to play with as he pleases. He can have a selection of toys of his own to chew on and play with whenever he likes. The toys used for training should not be included with these. They should belong to the owner who will determine where, when, and for how long they will be played with. This should mean that they will retain their novelty value in the dog's eyes.

Tug-type Toys

We prefer tug-type toys. For example, a ball on a rope where the owner can interact with the dog. Some people believe that tug-of-war games incite the dog to compete for leadership, as it can be a contest of strength. We believe that "tug" can become one of a dog's favorite games and, so long as the owner can stop the game with the dog relinquishing the toy on request, it can be of great benefit in training.

Whether using food or toys, similar principles apply. When first starting off, the reward may need to be very obvious, so you might hold it in your hand and it will be used very frequently. As you progress, it will still be used frequently but will be produced probably from your pocket. Ultimately, the toy or treat may become incidental because the good behavior patterns that you have been teaching will become second nature.

Toys or food may also be used as random rewards for especially good behavior or if teaching new exercises.

Right: This dog is waiting expectantly for his treat-reward after sitting promptly when asked.

Fetch

Many dogs have a basic instinct to chase a moving object. As puppies, this is motivated by curiosity and a desire to play. Even something as simple as a leaf blowing in the breeze will produce the reaction of chasing and pouncing. Nearly all puppies will pick up, or attempt to pick up, almost anything they find lying around the house or garden. If the item has an unpleasant taste or is painful to his mouth, he will probably abandon it. Everything else will either be played with and chewed, or presented for the owner's attention with a wagging tail and an expression that says "please play."

It is at this point that many owners inadvertently kill any inclination the dog may have had to give back the article to their hand. Instead, he discovers either that he should never have anything in his mouth because the owner screams and shouts, or he should hang on for grim death and run like hell.

Neither of these scenarios are an ideal response and almost certainly not what most owners would desire. The sensible reaction is to tell the puppy how clever he is, crouch down, and encourage him to bring it to you so that you can gently take it from him. Obviously, if every time he gives you his new toys, they are taken away and the game ends, he will soon stop allowing them to be taken from him. Therefore, do not just take the toy

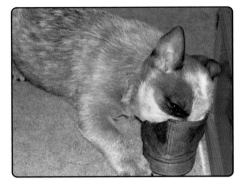

Above: Hopefully this is old footwear!

away: instead always praise him for bringing it to you, rewarding him with a game with one of his own toys or a treat.

Regardless of how valuable or fragile the item chosen as a toy by the puppy, try to keep calm and do not fall into the trap of chasing him. You might succeed in catching him while he is young, but he will get wise to any tricks and will get more difficult to catch. If you happen to see him about to pick up something inappropriate, by all means say "NO" then offer him an alternative.

Most puppies will learn to fetch farily easily if correctly encouraged from the start (*see pages 52–53*). Some of them, however, will have a tighter grip on the article than others. Try not to let him turn this into a fight game as you attempt to remove the item from his mouth. Usually if he sees another toy or a treat he will release his grip.

FETCH is fun and, once taught, great exercise for your dog when off the leash. Until he reliably comes back when called, this should always be taught on the leash.

"GOOD BOY, FETCH IT!"

1 CHASE THE TOY

Throw a toy that your dog likes a short distance so that he automatically chases it.

"GOOD BOY, COME"

2 ENCOURAGE WITH PRAISE

As he mouths it, encourage him with "**GOOD DOG, FETCH IT.**" Once he picks it up, walk back a few paces saying "**GOOD DOG, COME**" so that he bounces happily toward you.

3 A CLEAN TAKE

It is easier to take the toy cleanly if your dog will sit on request in front of you. At this stage you do not want your dog to decide to play tug of war or start chasing around. Gently start to take the article at the same time as telling him to leave it.

4 PRAISE OR PLAY

Praise him as he gives up the article. You can also teach your dog that if you use both hands to take the article, one either side of his mouth, you expect him to release it immediately, but if you use one hand only, it is an invitation to play tug.

NOTE: There are some dogs that show no interest in toys of any description. It may be possible to teach them to FETCH for competition, but they are unlikely to be enthusiastic about playing it.

CHAPTER 4

THE WEEKLY TRAINING PROGRAM

In this chapter we present our easy-to-follow dog training exercises. They build up on a week-by-week basis – the ten-week timescale coming from our considerable experience of running dog training courses with many different breeds and ages of dogs. If you follow and practice our exercises, step-by-step, then you and your dog should achieve a reasonable level of training by the end of the ten weeks.

No Worries
Do not worry if you feel you and your dog need more time on any particular aspect. It is a vital part of our training philosophy that you consolidate each piece of an exercise before you move on. We have therefore broken down our exercises into stages to help you and your dog to develop them successfully. They are very basic and there is no great trick to them, but they should help you have a more socially acceptable and responsive companion.

Daily Practice on the Leash
All practice needs to be carried out with the dog on a collar and leash, even indoors. Ideally, you should practice daily. Short, three or four ten-minute sessions are more beneficial than one long session. Start at a time and place where there are no distractions and you and your dog can concentrate.

As you join the stages together over the coming weeks, it is vitally important

Above: The timing of praise and reward provide a fundamental platform for our training exercises. Do not get so hung up on trying to teach your dog that you forget the simple but needed "Good Boy."

to always remember to praise your dog for each step correctly done, even if he needed help. The timing of the praise and reward is the most important part of any exercise. If the dog has sat well, but received the praise as he is getting up, he will think it is the getting up that is correct. Remember, you need a plan in your mind of what training you are going to do, as the dog has not got a clue.

Also beware of simply concentrating so hard on teaching that you end up just telling the dog what to do, and then forgetting the all-important praise. Our training is not about teaching exercises for the sake of it, it is endeavoring to build a partnership that will make life more pleasant for you and your dog.

Stand

CHECKLIST
- Ensure the collar is loose and leash already attached.
- Choose a quiet time and place.
- Wear loose-fitting clothes.
- Avoid distractions.

NOTE:
- STAND / SIT / DOWN can be useful taught together as it can help your dog understand the difference between them. Encourage your dog to stay beside you, and remain on the same spot.

Sit your dog at your left side. To put the dog in the stand, you should turn at a slight angle to face his side. Hold the leash quite short in the right hand, over the dog's back and low along his spine, with the collar loose. As you give the "STAND" command, slide your left hand (palm up) thumb toward his hind leg, underneath the dog on the side nearest to you and move it toward his back leg. When your dog stands praise him immediately.

1 HIND FEET BACKWARDS
Your dog should stand by moving his hind feet backward, not his front feet forward. If he attempts to move forward, check back along his spine with the leash, making sure the collar returns to being loose.

"STAND"
"GOOD BOY"

2 STOP HIS BACK SWINGING OUT
If he attempts to swing his back end out away from you, slide your left hand all the way underneath and bring him back to the starting position. Remind him to "STAND" and praise him immediately. In every step do not forget the praise.

(3) LEASH OVER THE BACK

Repeated regularly, the dog will soon learn. Then all you need to do is put the leash over his back, and as you slide your hand down and command, the dog should be standing. Praise him while you keep him standing still, and then release or move him to another position.

Above: Do not be in a hurry to move your left hand out from under the dog. Use it to tickle his tummy or just inside his hind leg. You do not need to pat the top of his head to praise him. If your dog is very ticklish on the tummy, or unduly anxious, then you could start with the dog against a wall; he will then be unable to swing away from you.

Above: Resist the urge to pick up your dog in a horseshoe fashion; otherwise, "STAND" will simply mean to him "mom's going to pick me up." Make sure he is properly balanced.

Sit

In teaching this exercise you are not just teaching your dog to sit, you are teaching him to do it quickly and close to your left leg. Many dogs learn to "SIT" on command easily, but they tend to want to face you. This can be very awkward if, for instance, your dog is on the leash and you are waiting on the pavement trying to cross the road or climb over a turnstile.

① DOG AT YOUR LEFT SIDE

Start with your dog in the "STAND" position at your left side. Hold your leash quite short in your right hand, left hand at the dog's left side, thumb across his back, and fingers by his groin.

"GOOD BOY"

② RIGHT HAND GUIDING

Command "SIT," and at the same time give a couple of checks up and back with the leash in your right hand while your left hand guides the dog into the "SIT" close by your left leg. His front feet should be level with yours. Make sure that the collar is loose but be ready to check again if necessary. Praise him immediately.

Above: Try to make sure that your left hand is correctly positioned over your dog's back as shown in Step 1. If you are tempted to use the hand position shown above, you may be able to help your dog to sit, but you will not be able to guide him in close to your left leg.

③ KEEPING THE CORRECT SIT POSITION

Do not be in a hurry to move your left hand away as he may try to jump up. Praise him while he remains sitting still and then release or move him back into the stand. You should always be ready to help him keep the correct position until you clearly indicate to him that he may move. Use your left hand to pat him low down on his flank, or your right hand to tickle his head and ears without losing control.

Above: If you have a very bouncy and/or strong-willed dog, you may find initially that you are exerting a lot of pressure to keep him in the "SIT." Try to get the praise in while he is sitting, even though he has no option but to remain sitting.

Down

This is one of the most important exercises to teach your dog. There can be many dangers which can come between him and you – calling him back toward you could put him in the line of danger, or he may just decide to run or cause an accident. If he will go down instantly, and wait for you to go to him, then he should be safe. We prefer to teach a dog to go down from the stand position because the likelihood is that the dog will be standing or moving. If he has to think about sitting first, he will go down too slowly and may move into the line of danger.

1 LEFT HAND PUSH

With your dog at your left side standing still, give the "DOWN" command, simultaneously move the leash in the right hand from over his spine down beside his right shoulder, and with your left hand, push down and diagonally back toward the hind feet.

2 HAND OVER RIDGE

The middle finger and thumb of your left hand should be locked onto the ridge above his shoulders. Do not let your hand slip while making this movement, or you will find the dog sitting rather than going straight down. On very smooth coated dogs, such as Boxers, this will need watching.

3 FOLDING DOWN

Your dog should "fold" easily into the down position, although you may need to apply quite steady pressure. Praise him immediately as he starts to go down. The right hand goes down with your dog, keeping the collar loose unless he attempts to resist; in this case a check down can be given.

4 STROKE THE BACK

Do not let him jump up straight away, praise him while he is still down, making sure the collar is loose. Stroke along the dog's back with your left hand, using light pressure that can be increased if he tries to move too soon. Wait until he is relaxed and then release him.

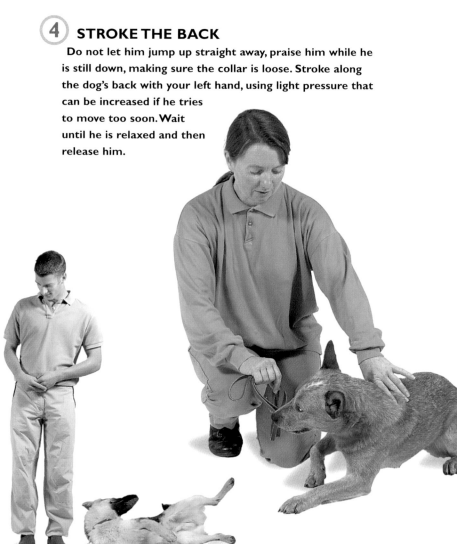

Above: Some dogs try to turn this exercise into a game by nibbling and chewing at your hands or arms. A useful tip is to put your foot on the leash to free your arms. Quickly and quietly put your left foot on the leash very close to the collar and stand up. This removes your hands and arms from his mouth and effectively ends the game. He may protest noisily, attempting to get up hind end first; but if you praise him, encouraging him to stay "DOWN," he will relax.

Right: Most puppies and young dogs will roll over onto their back or side, waving their feet in the air when placed in the down position. This is quite natural and should not be worried about. A dog lying with his feet in the air is not out of control.

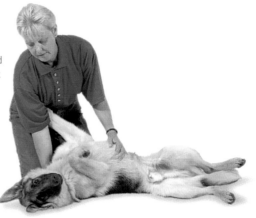

"GOOD BOY" **5 WAIT FOR RELEASE**

When he eventually relaxes, ease the tension on the leash, kneel down again, and praise him while he is down and release him. Your dog can be taught to go back up into the sit or stand positions from the down. However, we consider it safer if the dog remains down until you release him. If the dog has been told to go down in an emergency situation, he may be steadier if he is expecting you to rejoin him and release him.

Watch

If you can get your dog's attention, when you want it, then he will be listening and ready for what comes next. "WATCH" may also be useful if, for example, your dog has a piece of grass near his eye and you need to remove it. If he will look at you and let you stroke his face, you can remove the grass with minimal hassle.

"WATCH"

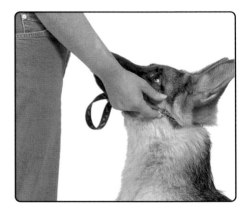

① CORRECT WATCH

Get the dog to sit in front of you, hook your fingertips under the collar at the back of his neck. Command **"DOG'S NAME," "WATCH"** in a pleasant tone. At the same time slide your hands around the collar on either side of the dog's neck up underneath the dog's muzzle.

② 2-SECOND EYE CONTACT

Stroke the sides of the dog's face with your thumbs and praise him. If you get the dog to make eye contact for two or three seconds the first time, that will be sufficient. Now release him.

Above: Do not grip the dog by the scruff of his neck to achieve the "WATCH" position. Your dog may feel that he is going to be told off and start to struggle. You will also find yourself unable to stroke the sides of the dog's face when giving praise.

3 BUILD A GAP

The praise must be while making eye contact. Gradually build up the length of time that he will watch you, until eventually all you need to do is give the command and he will look at you. Some dogs will hold the head position but avoid making eye contact. In this case try making squeaking noises and praise instantly when he looks; then release him.

Above: We are aiming for eye contact not nose contact. Your back should remain as upright as possible. If you are standing with a larger dog, your feet should be close to the dog's front feet, you may bend your knees if necessary but not your back.

"GOOD BOY"

① SMALL DOG WATCH

"WATCH"

With a very small dog you might have to kneel with him between your knees. You should remember to keep your back as straight as possible, the aim is to encourage the dog to look up to you. Have your dog sit in front of you, hook your fingertips underneath the collar at the back of the dog's neck. Command **"DOG'S NAME"** and **"WATCH"** in a pleasant tone.

At the same time slide your hands around the collar on either side of the dog's neck up underneath his muzzle and turn his head up encouraging him to make eye contact. In this position you should be able to stroke the sides of your dog's face with your thumbs, praising him at the same time. It's good if you get your dog to make eye contact for two or three seconds the first time; release him afterwards.

(2) CORRECT POSITION

"GOOD BOY"

Eventually you will be able to command **"DOG'S NAME"** and **"WATCH"** and he will automatically look up to make eye contact with you. The principal, and end position, is the same whether you have a small dog or a big dog, but your starting position is lower when you begin to teach this exercise to a small dog. Again, for those dogs that might hold the head position but avoid making eye contact, try making high squeaky noises to catch his eye and then praise the instant he looks.

Right: Leaning over like this is really only a good way to get back ache. Remember to try to keep your back straight and go for eye contact, not nose contact.

Long Down and Long Sit

These two exercises can be particularly useful if you have a boisterous or strong-willed dog. They are designed to make the dog realize that you are dominant over him without losing your temper or perhaps resorting to physical violence, which never achieves anything. The aim is to keep the dog "DOWN" for 30 minutes and in the "SIT" for ten minutes. It is important that these two exercises are not practiced consecutively: do the "LONG DOWN" one day and the "LONG SIT" the next. Pick the optimum time to do these exercises, both for yourself and the dog, particularly the "DOWN."

1 SETTLING DOWN

Start the "LONG DOWN" exercise when your dog is ready to settle down on his own accord for a rest. With the collar and leash on the dog, put him in the "DOWN" position, making sure he is comfortable.

2 FOOT ON THE LEASH

If he is relaxed then you can relax too – maybe watching television or having a cup of coffee, while keeping an eye on your dog. If he is restless, a foot on the leash may be required. Occasional praise may be given, especially if the dog is a little anxious, but it should not be a continuous fuss.

③ WHEN TO RELEASE

At the end of the time, if he is asleep, do not tiptoe off and leave him. Praise him while he is still "**DOWN**," then release. He may roll over and go back to sleep, that is okay, you have made clear that he has finished.

Left: If your dog tries to turn this into a game by chewing and nibbling at your hands and arms, remain calm. Slide your left foot up the leash, close to the collar as quickly as possible and stand up. As the dog settles, praise him and continue the exercise, releasing the tension as appropriate.

"GOOD BOY"

THE LONG SIT

The principle is exactly the same for the "**LONG SIT**" but it is only for ten minutes. Like the "**DOWN**," he has to sit and stay. If he moves put him back in the "**SIT**" position and start again. Try and ensure that the dog sits upright with his weight equally divided on both hips, not flopped to one side.

At the end of the time, praise him while he is still sitting and then release him.

Fast Down

The aim of this command is to put the dog in a "DOWN" position, as described in Week One, but to do it very quickly. Take care to keep your left hand on his shoulder ridge and your right hand going down beside his shoulder. Praise him while he is "DOWN," keep him there for a count of five and then release him.

CHECKLIST
- STAND/ SIT/ DOWN Practice these exercises as often as you can.
- WATCH With this command try and increase the time the dog is making eye contact.
- LONG SIT AND LONG DOWN Alternate these exercises every other day.
- Remember the praise.

① WALK IN A CIRCLE
If your dog is starting to go down quite quickly because of the pressure of your hand, start to walk him in a left hand circle.

② RIGHT HAND LEAD
Turn toward your dog, take the leash close to the clip with your right hand if it is not already there, and at the same time command "DOWN."

③ FIRM PRESSURE
Give the command before you put your left hand on top of his shoulders, using firm pressure to help him go down very quickly.

④ AVOID HAND SLIDING ON BACK OR NECK

Do not let your hand slide down his back or down his neck, because this would allow him to sit or put his chin on the ground with his bottom in the air. He should fold quickly, like a pack of cards. Remember to bring your right hand (which is holding the leash) down at the same time so that you do not strangle him.

"GOOD BOY"

⑤ RIGHT HAND LEASH

Praise immediately while he is down and then release. Do not put your hand on him before commanding; give him a second or two to do it himself, but do not wait too long and do not keep repeating the command. With practice he will realize that he should drop on the command before you touch him. This exercise should be repeated as often as possible. The more frequent the repetition, the faster the response will become.

Down Stay

If the dog has been going "DOWN" easily, has been praised while down, and has successfully completed "LONG DOWNS," this exercise should be easy. Do not use your dog's name before the "STAY" command, as this may encourage him to move.

"STAY" to the dog, should mean "You may relax, but do not change position or move from that spot; I will come back and release you." Keep an eye on him but do not stare. If you think that he is going to move, return immediately, even if you have not finished. Hopefully, he will not move and you will be able to praise him; alternatively you will be able to correct him quickly and remind him to "STAY."

1 SETTLING YOUR DOG DOWN

Place the dog in the "DOWN" as before, settling him so he is comfortable. If possible get him to roll on one hip as illustrated or, if he likes, flat on his side.

2 LAY DOWN THE LEASH

Using the leash on the long length, lay it on the ground to the right of the dog. Make sure the collar stays loose and that he does not get up.

③ VISUAL AND VERBAL STAY

Stand on the leash as close as possible to your dog; he should be settled, but if he is still trying to turn this into a game, you may need to keep tension on the leash until he has relaxed. Command "**STAY**" giving a visual command with the palm of your hand in front of his face.

"STAY"

④ STAND STRAIGHT AND COUNT TO FIVE

Stand up straight beside him, count to five, then bend down and quietly "**PRAISE**" him, patting him gently. Do not be too exuberant with your praise as you want your dog to remain calmly down; but he needs to know that he is doing the exercise correctly and you are pleased with him. Then either use your release command and let your dog get up, or command "**STAY**" and repeat the exercise.

5 PACING AWAY ON THE LEASH

Once you have him used to this and very settled, you can try a pace or two away from him. Move away to the right along the line of the leash so that you have control and he cannot get away from you.

6 STAND UPRIGHT

Stand upright, keeping an eye on your dog and count to five. If he looks like he is going to move, get back to him right away, even if you have not yet counted to five.

7 BACK ALONG THE LINE

After you have counted to five, return to the dog along the line of the leash. Try not to talk to the dog and stay upright, he is more likely to try and get up to greet you if you bend.

8 COUNT BEFORE RELEASING HIM

Stand upright beside him, but do not allow him to get up while you count to two. The reason for counting to two before you praise him is that if you fuss over him immediately upon your return, he is more likely to want to get up to meet you in anticipation that it is the end of the exercise. If he starts to get up, try and use tension with your foot on the leash to prevent it.

"GOOD BOY"

9 BEND DOWN AND PRAISE

After you have counted to two, bend down and praise him, making sure that he stays in the "**DOWN**" position. If he rolls on his back with his feet in the air while receiving the praise, this does not matter. Release him or settle him and repeat the exercise.

Stand

Out of the three positions, "STAND" can be the most difficult for a dog to learn. Standing on four feet is not a problem, standing still is, or can be! Always be ready to help him up and do not forget to make sure that he is balanced. Do not attempt to move your hands away until he is absolutely steady. This is an exercise that can be worked on while you are grooming the dog.

CHECKLIST
- STAND/SIT/DOWN Practice as often as you can.
- WATCH Continue to increase the time that the dog makes eye contact. Remember to praise while he is making eye contact, not after.
- LONG SIT AND LONG DOWN Alternate these exercises every other day.
- FAST DOWN Practice as in Week Two.
- DOWN STAY Practice as in Week Two.

① LEFT HAND POSITION

With your dog settled in the stand, keep your left hand under the tummy for a bitch, while with a male tickle just inside the hind leg. Lay the lead over the dog's back with your right hand as illustrated (with a small dog, lay the leash down on the ground).

② LEASH OVER BACK LIKE A SADDLE

Place the leash over the dog's back like a saddle so that it does not slip and distract him. Do not try to lie the leash along the length of the dog's spine. Remind him to stand, drop your left hand away, and stand upright and count to five. He should be keeping all four feet still. If he starts to fidget, pick up the leash, put your left hand back, and remind him to stand before trying again.

"GOOD BOY"

③ LEFT HAND TO DOG'S TUMMY

After you have counted to five, put your left hand back under his tummy while your right hand goes to pick up the leash. Praise him quietly while he is standing still and then release him or ask him to go into sit or down.

Watch from Side

Now that your dog is watching you from the front, you can begin to teach the "WATCH" from the side. The main use for this exercise is at the start of heelwork. If your dog is watching you then hopefully he is also paying attention and is less likely to be distracted by his surroundings. In the same manner as teaching the "WATCH" from the front, use a pleasant tone in your commands. Make sure you are not nagging. Most importantly, get the praise in while the dog is making eye contact, not as he looks away. Build the time up, using literally seconds at a time, as your dog's ability to concentrate increases.

"GOOD BOY"

WITH A LARGE DOG

Your dog should be sitting at your left side with the leash held in your right hand. Move your left hand over the top of the dog's head and slide it down so the fingertips are under the dog's jaw. Command "DOG'S NAME" and "WATCH" in a pleasant tone, while turning his head up against your body to make eye contact. Praise him as he does this, then release him or repeat the step.

WITH A SMALL DOG

The principle is the same with a small dog, but obviously you will need to bend lower. Try to bend sideways, sliding your left hand down your left leg rather than leaning forward to obstruct the dog's view.

"WATCH"

WITH EXPERIENCE

Practiced enough, you should eventually be able to command **"DOG'S NAME"** and **"WATCH"** and have him turn his head up to make eye contact with you. When teaching this exercise, it can be useful to exaggerate the upward tilt of the head to help the dog understand what is required. Once your dog has learned the exercise, the tilt may not be so marked, but the eyes will still make contact.

Heelwork

You must teach HEELWORK on a slack leash and loose collar. Your dog cannot learn if the leash is tight. While you may be able to keep him by your side with physical strength, this will not teach him anything. Some dogs are very good at not quite pulling but still keeping the leash just taut; they can feel where their owner is and so do not have to look or listen.

① SITTING AND WATCHING

Have your dog in the "SIT" at your left side watching you. As he sits and watches you, praise each action. Allow 4–6in (10–15cm) of slack leash.

"HEEL," "GOOD BOY"

② LEFT LEG AND LEFT HAND

The leash will probably have been in your right hand as you helped the dog "SIT" and "WATCH." Just before stepping off, transfer it to your left hand. Command "DOG'S NAME" and "HEEL" and step off smartly with the left leg; then praise immediately.

③ HOOK THUMB IN TROUSERS

Ideally, hold the leash in your left hand only and position your hand in front of your left leg. Try hooking your thumb into your trouser pocket to achieve the correct position.

4 USING BOTH HANDS

With a particularly strong dog, you may need to hold the leash in both hands. Remember, keep the collar loose on your dog's neck. Think of the leash as a teaching aid not a tow rope for the dog to pull.

5 SIX TO TEN PACES

Step off in a positive manner. Praise the dog immediately. Do not wait for him nor should you check him forward. If he does not move quickly with you, he will check himself. Walk in a left hand circle at a brisk pace, aiming for six to ten paces with the dog in the correct position, all the time praising and reminding him to "HEEL."

6 STEP BACK TO RELEASE YOUR DOG

Now release the dog by taking a pace backward. Use your dog's name so that he turns toward you for the praise.

7 DO NOT SAY ANYTHING

If at some stage the dog moves out of the correct heelwork position by pulling forward or sideways, do not say anything. The leash is going to tell the dog that he is not doing what you want.

8 MOVE HAND TO LEASH FOR MORE SLACK

You must move your hand toward the dog wherever it is in order to give more slack in the leash. It is no good letting the leash lengthen out, as it will still be tight. You cannot check on a tight leash; you can only pull.

⑨ FIRM CHECK

Check in the opposite direction to that which your dog is moving. The check should be firm enough to get him back in the correct position by your left leg with a loose collar – so you can praise him.

"GOOD BOY, HEEL"

⑩ REPEAT CHECK

Check as often as necessary. Remember not to speak as you check. It is more important to get the praise in as the dog returns to your side. Hopefully he will look at you as you praise him; then you can remind him **"HEEL."**

"GOOD BOY"

REWARDING YOUR DOG

If your dog is walking nicely to heel, do not be afraid to give him the occasional pat preferably with your right hand because moving your left hand may push him away from you. Talk to him if he is paying attention to you so that he knows you are pleased with him. If you are using food as a reward, the occasional treat produced from your right hand pocket will reinforce this. Keep it fun; intersperse short bursts of correct heelwork with time out for a quick game.

Sit in Heelwork

CHECKLIST

- STAND as in the previous week, but increase the count to ten or twelve.
- SIT Practice as often as you can.
- DOWN Practice as often as you can.
- WATCH Practice at the front and side. Aim for longer periods of attention.
- LONG SIT AND LONG DOWN If your dog is still unsettled in these exercises, continue alternating every other day.
- FAST DOWN Continue left hand circles, helping your dog to go down as quickly as possible.
- DOWN STAY Continue as in Week Three, but move three paces forward off the leash and count to ten. Stand sideways to your dog so that you can keep an eye on him – do not face him directly.
- HEELWORK Left hand circles only – concentrate on getting the dog to stay happily at your left side on a slack leash.
- Remember always to help the dog get it right so you can praise him, and praise him as often as you can.

For the SIT IN HEELWORK, it is vital you do not suddenly stop. While you may know you are going to stop, your dog has no idea, and if you stop suddenly the dog will already be the length of the leash in front of you.

① NO SUDDEN HALTS

While moving with your dog, transfer the leash to the right hand. Do not stop suddenly.

② HAND CLOSE TO THE TRIGGER HOOK

You must try and get your hand as near to the trigger hook as possible, as this will help you control where the dog sits. This may be more difficult with a small dog, but it is important because it helps you keep him close and makes it easier to help him into the correct sit position.

"SIT"

"WATCH"

③ LEFT HAND HELPS INTO SIT

Command "SIT" and use your left hand to help your dog into the sit as you stop (as you have already practiced in the stationary position). Praise your dog while he is sitting and encourage him to "WATCH." Then either continue HEELWORK or release him.

Sit in Heelwork: big dog

① LESS BENDING FOR A BIG DOG

The exercise is the same whether the dog is small or large. Obviously, you do not need to bend so far to reach the clip on the leash with a big dog, but it is just as important as it helps with control.

② THUMB AND FINGERS

Resist the temptation to bend over your dog; instead, try and stay as upright as possible. Bend your knees, if necessary, while your right hand is checking up and slightly back and your left hand is ready to help him into the "SIT." Thumb over the dog's back with you fingers flat against his groin as illustrated.

③ STAY BALANCED

The command "SIT" should be given as you stop. It is important to make sure that you are balanced, probably with feet slightly apart, so that you do not fall over your dog as you put him in the sit. Then use your left hand to guide him in to sit close to your left leg. Remember to keep your thumb over his back and your fingers flat against him, not digging into him. His front feet should be level with your feet and facing the same direction.

"SIT"

"GOOD BOY"

④ AVOID ANY LEAPING UP

Praise your dog as he sits, and do not let him leap up – you may need to keep your left hand in position while you praise him. It is okay if he is leaning on your left leg. Then either release or ask him to **"WATCH"** and continue **HEELWORK**.

Sit Stay

Your dog must be steady in the "SIT" position before you attempt the "SIT STAY." If he is not steady when you are standing next to him, he certainly will not let you take a pace away. Do not rush this exercise; the more time you take the steadier he will be. It is very important that you praise gently and calmly: being exuberant in your praise is likely to make your dog move. Some dogs initially worry when their owner disappears for a second behind them and tend to leap up. If this habit is persistent with your dog, you should do a half circle in front of the dog, walking backward to the starting point. The arc can be gradually increased until it is a full circle.

① DOG ON LEFT WITH LONG LEASH

Start with your dog at the left side in the "SIT" position. The leash should be at the long length, not clipped up short.

"SIT"

② RIGHT HAND SIGNAL

Command "STAY" in a pleasant but firm tone; at the same time, using your right hand, give a visual command with the palm of your hand in front of your dog's face.

3 CORRECT GRIP ON LEASH

Take the end of the leash in your right hand. With the flat of your left hand, palm, take up the slack in the leash over the dog's head.

"GOOD DOG"

"STAY"

4 HAND NOT TOO HIGH

Do not have your hand too high up in the air, as you will be unable to correct the dog if he moves, but do make sure the collar is loose. Step one pace to the right.

5 CIRCLING YOUR DOG

If your dog is steady, move slowly forward and around the dog in a circle. Remind him **"GOOD DOG" "STAY,"** if necessary, in a pleasant tone of voice.

"SIT STAY"

6 CHECK UPWARD

If he moves or starts to fidget, check upward with the left hand and remind him to **"SIT STAY,"** and praise if he does. Try and correct at arm's length rather than going right back to him.

"GOOD BOY"

7 WATCH WHILE ON THE MOVE

Keep your eye on the dog all the time you are moving. It is better to remind him to **"SIT STAY"** and praise gently rather than letting him move and then correcting him.

8 KEEPING THE RIGHT PACE

Use a nice steady pace; do not rush or the dog may startle. Also, do not go too slowly or he may think you are teasing him. As you get back with your dog's right shoulder, take a step to the left so you are close beside him where you started.

9 COUNT TO TWO

Stand by his side, count to two, and then praise him gently without letting him move. Some dogs will try and slide into the "DOWN;" be ready to check and remind him to "SIT." Try not to let him spoil the exercise by making a mistake at the end of it. Then either repeat or release him.

Fast Down

You now need to start building up the distance between you and your dog. Ask someone to help you, give the leash to them, and have them walk the dog away from you – no more than 6.5ft (2m).

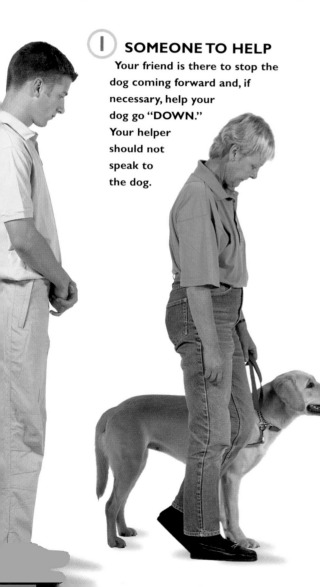

① SOMEONE TO HELP
Your friend is there to stop the dog coming forward and, if necessary, help your dog go "DOWN." Your helper should not speak to the dog.

CHECKLIST
- STAND As before, if the dog is steady command STAND stepping off with the right foot. Move two paces in front of the dog. Turn and go straight back to his side, keep him standing still while praising gently. Then either repeat or release.
- SIT Practice as often as you can.
- DOWN Practice often.
- WATCH Practice at front and side aiming for longer periods of attention.
- LONG SIT AND LONG DOWN If you have a very bouncy or strong-willed dog, it is worth continuing with these exercises.
- DOWN STAY Put the dog in the down as before, lay the leash on the ground stretched out to the right. Command DOWN, STAY. Take one pace to the right along the leash and then five paces forward. Standing sideways to your dog, count to 15 and return to your dog as previously described.
- HEELWORK Continue with left hand circles, including quick, close SITS at the halt. Then start doing straight lines with the dog in the SIT position at the start and halt, watching.

2 COMMAND DOWN

As dog and helper turn to face you, command "**DOWN**." Do not say his name and try not to bend as this will encourage the dog to come toward you. If necessary, clap your hands or stamp your foot to get your dog's attention. This should only be done when you are first attempting this exercise to give the dog every opportunity to succeed.

3 HAND SIGNAL IS FINE

Using a hand signal is acceptable so long as you do not bend. Some people prefer to use a hand-up-in-the-air signal, which they feel will be seen better from a distance, but most people automatically point down as they command.

"DOWN"

4 HELPING HAND

If he does not go down, repeat the command "**DOWN**." The person holding the leash should use their left hand on the dog's shoulder to put your dog into the "**DOWN**."

5 FOCUSED DOG

Tell him "**GOOD BOY STAY DOWN**" and get back to him quickly and quietly. Your friend should make sure the dog does not get up, avoiding fussing and eye contact with him, so as to keep your dog's attention focused on you.

6 NO OVERBENDING

You should return in an upright stance as any premature bending almost certainly will encourage the dog to try and leap up. When reaching the dog, you should go down to him to praise him.

"GOOD BOY"

7 PRAISE AND PAT

Your friend/helper should not be involved in fussing with the dog. You must make sure that the dog receives his praise and patting while still in the down position. When you are ready you can release the dog. This exercise should be repeated frequently. If the dog is responding well in a quiet situation, then it can be practiced when there are distractions.

"GOOD BOY STAY DOWN"

Sit Stay

Your dog should be quite relaxed and steady while you are circling around him slowly. If not, more work needs to be done on that basic part of the exercise. Always remember to praise him for the parts done correctly: this includes the initial "SIT" before attempting a clear "STAY" command. As with the "DOWN STAY," do not use the dog's name, as this is likely to make him move. The praise must be given calmly not over-excitedly, but enough to let the dog know you are pleased with him.

1 A SMALL PACE TO THE RIGHT

Command "STAY." Take a small pace to the right and then return immediately to his side. Count to two before praising him quietly and then remind him to "STAY."

2 TO THE END OF THE LEASH

This time move out to the right to the end of the leash and then return immediately. Keep a nice steady, confident speed, and do not move too quickly nor too slowly. Praise the dog quietly as before and remind him to "STAY."

③ SMALL STEP TO THE RIGHT

Next, take a small step to the right and walk out in front of the dog to the end of the leash. Keep an eye on your dog all the time in case he thinks about moving.

"GOOD BOY"

④ BACK TO DOG'S SIDE

Do not stand and stare at the dog, but return immediately to the dog's side, praising as previously described. Always remember to praise your dog for the parts that are done correctly. This includes the initial **"SIT"** before attempting a clear **"STAY"** command. Then either repeat the exercise or release the dog.

Front Present

This exercise is part of teaching your dog to come instantly when called in a controlled manner. The emphasis should be on the command "COME" and the praise. In order for this to develop into a reliable habit off-leash, it is essential that the praise be enthusiastic and genuine and that the leash and collar remain loose. It can be practiced any time the dog is on the leash and is distracted—for example, when he is watching other dogs or joggers. It does not always have to be set up as a formal exercise.

"COME"

1 STRAIGHT AHEAD

Walk in a straight line with the dog at heel; ideally the leash should be held in the left hand only ready for the next step. Do not allow the leash to lengthen by sliding through your hand.

2 BACK STEP

Call your "**DOG'S NAME**" and command "**COME**." Bend slightly and extend your arm. Check with the leash and walk backward on the same line at a steady pace; do not attempt to run.

3 LEASH UNDER CHIN

Praise your dog as he turns to face you and keep the leash low so that it is under his chin. Do not try and push your dog forceably away from you – step back away from him and he will have to turn toward you.

"GOOD BOY, COME"

4 HANDS AS TARGETS

Praise your dog and remind him to "COME" as you continue to move back another few paces; his attention should be totally focused on you. Keep your hands together low down – these should be the target your dog is coming toward.

⑤ ENCOURAGE TOWARD YOU

Make sure the leash and collar are loose. If your dog attempts to go past you, check and encourage him to come straight in front. Viewed from the side, note that the dog is pushing his nose into his owner's hands and that the collar and leash are loose and low under his chin. The dog is being encouraged in; he is not being reeled in like a fish on the end of a line.

6 COMING TO A STOP

To help your dog come in straight, you may find it useful to walk backward with your feet slightly apart so that the dog is not treading on your toes. Once the dog is coming in straight, you can prepare to stop.

"GOOD BOY"

HAND UNDER THE CHIN

As you stop, make sure you are balanced, especially with a big dog who may knock you over. Just before you stop, grip your dog's collar under his chin with your left hand to help guide him in and keep his head up. Do not worry about the leash; it can stay in the same hand or you can let it drop once you have hold of the collar.

8 BRING HEAD UP

Keeping your grip on his collar under his chin with your left hand, bring your dog's head up as you command "**SIT**." At the same time use your right hand on his bottom to help him sit close in front. Try to do this smoothly in an all-in-one movement without grabbing and pushing the dog around.

"SIT"

"WATCH"

9 REINFORCE THE REWARD

Once your dog is sitting in front of you, ask him to "**WATCH**." Praise him warmly. If you are occasionally using a treat or toy to reinforce the reward, now is a good time to produce it from your pocket. Toys and treats should be an added bonus that the dog hopes he will get, but does not always receive. This usually helps keep him interested and happy to return to his owner.

About Turn in Heelwork

When you change direction you must let your dog know. For the "ABOUT TURN," you turn to the right and use the "DOG'S NAME" in a pleasant tone, as if you were calling him. This should encourage him to look up at you and help him come around. Remember also that it is important to look where you are going as this alters your body posture, giving the dog a clear signal of the change of direction. You might try practicing this to begin with using a line on, say, an empty car park or tennis court.

① DON'T LOOK DOWN

Use your dog's name and slow down slightly, but do not look down at the dog as this will tend to push him back.

③ STAY ON THE LINE

Once you are out of the turn, replace your left hand to your normal heelwork position and return to normal walking pace. Two points to remember: your left hand should remain in contact with your body as you make the turn and you must try and return on the same line as you walked up, not in a horseshoe shape.

"GOOD BOY"

DOG

HANDLER

② SLIDE YOUR LEFT HAND ACROSS

Turn your head to look the way you want to go and slide your left hand across your body to the right, not up. Aim to reach as far as your right hand trouser or skirt pocket. This will take up the slack in the leash so your dog stays close as he turns. Remember to praise.

CHECKLIST

- STAND As before, if your dog is steady command STAND, step off with the right foot and move four paces in front of your dog. Turn sideways onto him, count to five, and then go back to his side. Keep him standing still, praising gently, then release.
- SIT AND DOWN Practice as often as you can.
- WATCH Increase the period of attention.
- LONG SIT AND LONG DOWN Continue as needed.
- DOWN STAY As before but now take ten paces forward and then count to 15 before returning to your dog.
- SIT STAY With your dog in the sit position at your left hand side, command STAY and place the leash on the floor. Move one pace to the right and two paces to the front, count to five, and return to your dog.

Fast Down

By now your dog should be going down instantly when told, so now is the time to practice this exercise outside with some distractions. Do not be tempted to try this with the dog off the leash; because if he refuses, you may be unable to enforce it and he will learn that he can ignore your command. If you have someone to help, proceed with the exercise as described in Week Five. In this exercise you should be concentrating on the "DOWN" at a distance, not the "STAND;" therefore try and settle the dog quickly in the stand and walk away. Just the fact that you have walked away will usually keep the dog's attention and position, especially if you keep telling him "GOOD DOG, STAND."

(I) TIE THE LEASH

If you do not have a helper then tie your dog up on a long leash, making sure it is tied low down; you may need to use two leashes if one is not long enough.

(2) COMMAND STAND

Command the dog to "STAND" and position the leash as you have been doing in the "STAND" exercise. Now step off with the "RIGHT" foot.

3 TAKE SIX PACES

Walk about six paces out in front of your dog and turn to face him. Command "**DOWN**," remembering not to use his name as this will encourage him to move forward. If at any stage he does not go down instantly, you should return promptly to him and insist.

4 GET BACK

When he goes down tell him "**GOOD BOY, STAY**" and get back to him. If he gets up as you are returning, stand still and command "**DOWN**" again and continue.

5 PRAISE ON THE DOWN

Praise him, keeping him in the down until you are ready. Then give your "**RELEASE**" command and let him up.

Fast Down

Your dog should go "DOWN" instantly when told, even faster now after another week's work. You should still be working on building up the distance, but the stand should be improving as well. If you do not have anyone to assist, then repeat the exercise as in Week Six.

CHECKLIST

● WATCH Continue building up the time at front and side.

● DOWN STAY Put the dog down. Remove the leash putting it away in your pocket or around your body. Command STAY, take a small pace to the right, ten paces forward, and count to 15. Return to your dog, clipping your leash on while he is still down and while praising him, then release.

● SIT STAY With the dog in the SIT position at the left hand side, remove the leash, and put it in your pocket or around your body. Command STAY, take a small pace to the right and two paces to the front. Turn sideways onto the dog, count to five, and return to him. Make sure the dog remains in the SIT while you praise him and clip his leash on, then release.

1 WITH AN ASSISTANT

Place your dog in the "STAND," taking time to get him settled: only when he is settled should you pass the leash back to your assistant. Your helper must not distract your dog but can help by making sure the collar stays loose.

2 HAND SIGNALS

Remind your dog to "STAND," using your right hand to give a signal; your left hand can stay under his tummy until the last moment.

3 DOG'S ATTENTION ON YOU

Step off with your right foot, keeping an eye on your dog as you move. The dog's attention should be focused on you, not on the assistant.

4 KEEPING YOUR DOG STANDING

Your helper may also gently put her left hand under the dog's tummy to keep your dog standing if he has started to anticipate the exercise and tries to go down too soon. If he does anticipate – do not yell at him. Quietly reposition and try again with the aid of the helper. Walk out in front of the dog, turn to face him, and command "**DOWN.**" Remember to increase the distance over the course of the week.

5 DOWN FAST

He should go down immediately. Tell him "**GOOD DOG, STAY,**" and get back to him. If he does not go down, the helper should help him. Remember to praise him while he is still down before releasing him.

"GOOD DOG, STAY"

Right Turn in Heelwork

You should still be practicing straight lines and about turns with sits at the start and finish most of the time. Sometimes just release your dog by calling your "DOG'S NAME" and taking a pace backward, as when you started "HEELWORK" in Week Three. Practice left and right hand circles also incorporating "FRONT PRESENTS." Rather than doing circles all the time, you should now be seeking to teach your dog to do a proper right angle turn. The "RIGHT TURN" is executed in much the same way as the "ABOUT TURN."

1 SLOW UP SLIGHTLY

Slow up very slightly so that you give your dog enough time to come around with you, especially if you have a small dog. It can help to use slightly smaller steps rather than large ones to help your dog keep the correct **HEELWORK** position.

② LOOK AND SLIDE THE HAND

Turning your head to look the way you want to go, call your "**DOG'S NAME**" in a pleasant tone and slide your left hand across your body to the right to take up the slack in the leash. Make sure you keep your hand in contact with your body and that your hand slides across your body, not upwards.

Remember to praise your dog.

③ LEFT HAND POSITION

As you come out of the turn, replace your left hand to your normal **HEELWORK** position and return to a normal pace, praising your dog and reminding him to "**HEEL**."

Wait for Recall

Only if the "SIT STAY" is reliable should you start this exercise. If the "SIT STAY" is not steady then continue with "FRONT PRESENTS" incorporated in heelwork. Never practice this exercise immediately before or after a "SIT STAY" because it will cause the dog to become confused and you will almost certainly lose your "SIT STAY." We are going to try and make this exercise as different to a "SIT STAY" as possible. We are only going to use "SIT" as the command because we are going to ask the dog to move. Do not use his name until then. Concentrate on praising quietly and reminding him to "SIT."

① SIT AT LEFT HAND SIDE

Your dog should be put in the "SIT" position at the left hand side. Make sure that he is settled and preferably not flopped on one hip.

② LENGTHEN THE LEASH

Unclip the leash onto the long length, making sure that the collar stays loose and your dog does not move out of the "SIT."

3 LEFT HAND WORK

Hold all of the leash in the left hand, praising the dog and reminding him to "**SIT**." Remember not to use his name as you do not want him to move until you are ready.

4 MOVE CLOSE IN

Using a hand signal with the verbal command, start to move close in front of your dog.

5 FACE YOUR DOG

Facing your dog, remind him to "SIT," keeping a loose leash. Hold the dog's attention by saying "GOOD DOG, SIT" in a firm but pleasant tone—remember no name.

6 SLOWLY BACK OFF

Start to move confidently backward, to the end of the leash. Maintaining the hand signal may help keep your dog sitting. As you pay the leash out smoothly, ensure your dog's collar stays loose, with no tension on the leash.

"GOOD DOG, SIT"

7 MOVE STEADILY

Move at a steady pace, not too fast nor too slow as if teasing, keeping his attention by continually telling him "GOOD DOG, SIT." If your dog looks like he is going to move, then go straight back to settle him.

8 COUNT TO TWO

When you get to the end of the leash, stand still and count to two. The dog's attention should still be focused on you.

9 END OF THE LEAD

Bend slightly, extending the arm with the leash in preparation for checking and calling.

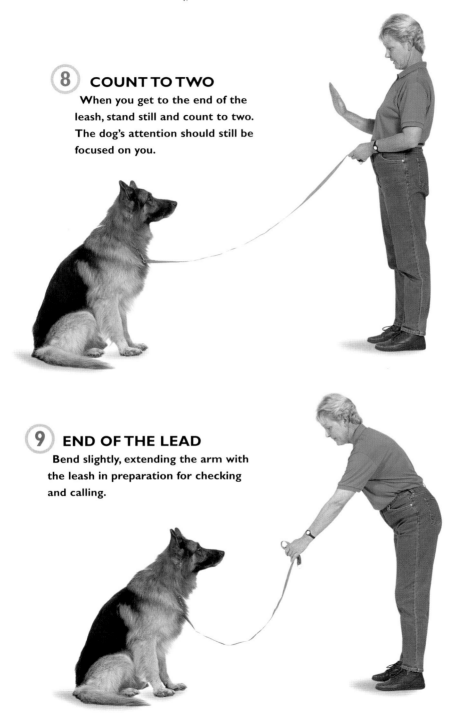

10 CHECK TO THE LEASH

As you command "DOG'S NAME," "COME," give a check to the leash, which should be sufficient to make the dog move immediately.

"COME"

11 PRAISE

As soon as he starts to get up to come to you, praise him. Do not be frightened to let him know how pleased you are with him.

12 RIGHT HAND HELP

Place your left hand in the collar, as in "FRONT PRESENT" (Week Five) and use your right hand to help him into the "SIT" in front of you.

"GOOD BOY"

(13) PRAISE REPEATED

Praise him while he is sitting and watching. Then repeat the first part of the exercise. However, instead of calling your dog out of the "**SIT**" position, return to him and praise him for sitting still. This will stop him anticipating that he will always be called out of the "**SIT**."

(14) RETURN TO HIS SIDE

Turn to stand back by his side, praising again before releasing.

Left Turn

To try a proper right-angle "LEFT TURN" in the heelwork, your dog needs to stop momentarily as you make the turn. His head and shoulder should stay by your left leg.

CHECKLIST
- STAND Increase to eight paces and count to ten.
- WATCH Practice front and side positions. He should be starting to respond to the word WATCH before you put your hands on him.
- LONG SIT AND LONG DOWN Continue if necessary (i.e. if dog is still rebellious).
- FAST DOWN Walk out 12 paces in front of the dog.
- DOWN STAY Increase to 30 seconds away from dog. SIT STAY Take five paces to the front and count to ten.
- RECALL Do not attempt this off the leash. If he gets away from you, you have undone all your hard work. Perhaps try a longer leash.
- HEELWORK Practice heelwork with your dog in the SIT at the start and halt, including ABOUT TURNS, RIGHT TURNS, and FRONT PRESENTS.

5 **NORMAL PACE**
Then return to a normal pace. Some sensitive dogs may over-react initially, so keep their confidence with praise.

1 **SMOOTH START**
When making the "LEFT TURN," the speed will vary depending on the type of dog you have, but try to make your hand movement as smooth as possible that your dog does not need to be checked.

4 LEFT HAND POSITION

Praise your dog and replace your left hand to the normal heelwork position as you step out of the turn.

3 BACK

At the same time command "**BACK**;" turn your head in the direction you want to go and execute the turn.

"BACK"

2 REPOSITION THE LEASH

Slide the leash around behind your back with your left hand, keeping it in contact with your body. This stops your dog from moving forward.

Polishing Off...

CHECKLIST

- **STAND** As in Week Seven, increase to 15 paces away and count to ten.
- **SIT AND DOWN** Practice often.
- **WATCH** Continue practicing FRONT and SIDE positions.
- **FAST DOWN** The dog should be steady in the STAND, so remove the leash, proceed as in Week Seven. If the dog moves forward, then go back to having a friend hold the leash or tie the dog up.
- **DOWN STAY** As in Week Seven, except increase the time to one minute away from your dog.
- **HEELWORK** As in Week Eight, but now incorporating LEFT TURNS.
- **SIT STAY** As in Week Seven, except take ten paces to the front, increase time to half a minute away from the dog.
- **RECALL** If the dog is steady in the SIT and is coming promptly to sit in front in response to your command, then try this exercise off-leash in a secure place outside. If in doubt use a long line instead of the leash.

By now you should have noticed an improvement in your dog's behavior, even though he may still have good days and bad days. This is quite normal: the extent of the improvement will depend on all the variables mentioned at the start of the book.

Where You and Your Dog Should Be after Completing the Course

Your dog should at least be doing all the exercises at home in a quiet environment with no distractions – if not, he needs considerably more time and effort spent on him. Be honest with yourself: have you really practiced as often as you should have? If the answer is no, then you know what to do. If the answer is yes then perhaps you have either a slow-thinking dog: so be patient; or a more dominant dog: so be consistently firm.

Venturing Outside

If he is doing the exercises nicely at home, then you can reasonably expect a good response elsewhere. Do not make excuses or give repeat commands if he does not respond promptly. Help him get it right so that you can praise him. Always expect him to be distracted in new surroundings and be

Left: This well-behaved dog is sitting under control while the handler feeds the ducks. Three distractions at once – food, something to chase, and a pond.

Above: No-one likes unruly dogs in a park – especially picnickers. This well-behaved dog is walking past on a loose leash while the picnickers' dog practices his long down.

prepared to enforce each command; then you can be pleasantly surprised if he does it correctly first time and you will be ready to praise him.

Your dog should have a good grasp of all the basic exercises by Week Ten – "STAND," "SIT," "DOWN," "WATCH," "LONG SIT," "LONG DOWN," "FAST DOWN," "DOWN STAY," "HEELWORK," "SIT STAY," and "RECALL."

Never be surprised if he does not respond as reliably in a strange place or with unusual distractions. Do not lose your temper and always be prepared to go back to the first steps if there is a problem. As before, do not make excuses and do not give repeat commands if he does not respond promptly. The key is to help him get it right so that you can praise him, and the greater variety of surroundings you can practice in, the more dependable he will become.

Everyday Routine Should Include Exercises for Your Dog

Try to make every effort to find opportunities for using your training exercises in your daily life with your dog. For example, you can use "STAND" when grooming your dog, drying his feet after a walk, or to check him over for grass in the summer—not to mention when you take him to the vet. "WATCH" can be used as his face is examined. "SIT" or "DOWN" can be practiced at dinner time, when you put his leash and collar on, going in and out of the car, or to stop him pushing first through doorways.

As we have stressed throughout, training should be fun for you and your dog. It should be possible to

Above: Dogs should always be kept under control around livestock. This dog is a good example of sitting quietly with a loose leash despite the curious cows.

Problems with RECALL

Perhaps the most common problem we encounter is the dog that will not come back when called. Our training exercises are designed to troubleshoot this problem, but some dogs still need further work. Hopefully, you will have followed our advice already in this book by not standing and continually shouting your dog's name and "COME" when it cannot be enforced. All this does is contradict the on-leash training and show your dog that he does not have to come instantly.

There is no doubt that some dogs need a lot more work on the

incorporate training sessions in your daily outings with your dog. They do not have to be formal sessions as such. So making the dog "SIT" before he is told to jump in the car for a ride to the supermarket or park can be used as a training exercise. The ride is part of the reward for most dogs.

Continue to incorporate training with everyday activities: do not just let him leap out to run crazy when you get to the park. He should "SIT" or "DOWN" until you tell him that he may get out. Indeed, it would not hurt to ask for a few minutes of obedience before starting his walk. Stopping with the dog in the "SIT" at every kerb emphasizes that you are leading, and the dog can be rewarded with a treat as well as a word of praise. Then continue moving, which is a reward in itself for most dogs.

Below: Not all parks welcome dogs, and some will only allow them on leashes. Even other dog owners do not always want to be jumped on by strange dogs, friendly or otherwise, so there can be plenty of opportunities to work with distractions. In reality training is never finished.

"RECALL" command than others. A totally unreliable dog is a danger to itself and others and should not be allowed freedom. He needs a lot more work on an increasingly long leash or line recalling it from various distractions. Remember to give enthusiastic praise and reinforce this with a treat or a game with a toy. Once your dog is returning promptly when called without the need for a check, despite the distraction, it may be time to try him off-leash in a secure place. He should be recalled many times during the course of the walk and be given a variety of rewards with the praise.

The standard of "HEELWORK" you require will differ depending on what you are now going to do with it. Although we have taught proper left and right turns, these probably will not

Above: Although this dog is off the leash, the value of the owner's "special" toy and attention outweigh the attraction of the other dogs.

be needed on a country stroll. Nevertheless, teaching close heelwork should have impressed on the dog that he should stay close to you whichever way you turn when he has been asked to "HEEL."

Training Is an On-going Process
Just because your dog does an exercise correctly once, it does not mean that he has learned that exercise. So keep using your training aids and never take unnecessary chances, however well-trained you feel he is. Always think safety first. Accidents happen, doors get left open for example, so if he will go down instantly on "FAST DOWN," it could save his life. "SIT STAY" and "DOWN STAY" can be used when you do not want him moving around, for whatever reason. While the training intensity may diminish, the practice should be on-going.

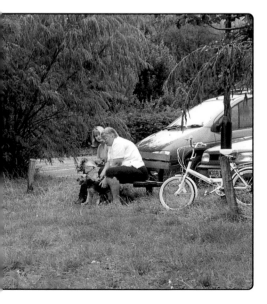

After the Training Course

Assuming that you have successfully completed your ten weeks training and are happy with the standard of control, now is the time to increase distractions and introduce new locations. Never be afraid to go back to the first steps of an exercise if your dog is experiencing difficulties or is distracted by new surroundings. Keep using your training aids: off-leash practice will come at a later stage.

Continue the Exercises

Continue regular practice sessions. Go over in your mind what you are going to do so that you can move from one exercise to another smoothly, without your dog sitting at the end of a leash waiting for you to reach a decision and getting bored in the process. If during an exercise you suddenly realize you are doing it incorrectly, then finish off as best you can. It is extremely important that every practice session ends on a good note with you and the dog in a happy frame of mind. Remember always to help the dog get it right so you can praise him.

Staying Positive Throughout

There are always variations but the fundamental principles of training have not really changed in practice. Some have acquired fancy sounding names, but it would be true to say that training methods, as we have shown in this book, have become much more positive. The emphasis is now on teaching rather than punishing. If the method you are using works, do not try and change it. If you have followed our training methods and have at least given thought to where possible problems may occur, those problems can usually be forestalled.

Competing

If you have an interest in perhaps entering competitions you will need to learn and teach the dog more polished and precise work. There are many different areas and levels of competition for the competitively minded dog owner. These range from Exemption Shows, which often have Breed and Obedience Classes (as well as Novelty Classes) and can be entered on the day of the show, to Championship Obedience or Working Trials Competitions or even Flyball or Agility, all of which have to be entered in advance. The latest competition is "Heelwork to Music," which is becoming tremendously popular.

Dog Training Clubs

A good place to start looking for more information and experience are the local dog training clubs. Contact can usually be made via the Telephone Directory, local veterinary establishments, the Kennel Club, pet

Right: Competitive Working Trials are based on police dog training and cover a number of exercises, including tracking. The dog tracks in a harness and with a long line rather than a lead. This dog's nose is well down as he follows the scent of the track layer.

supply shops, local newspapers, and word of mouth from fellow dog walkers. It is usually advisable to visit all the possible clubs, preferably in the first instance without your dog, so that you can look and listen to what is being said and done. Only if you are happy with the methods used and the experience available should you ask to join. Some clubs are aimed entirely at pet obedience and will be of no real benefit if you wish to compete; but they can be great fun and an opportunity for both you and your dog to socialize.

If It Does Not Work Out...

Some dogs can be more difficult to train than others. The reasons are many, ranging from breed and age to temperament and background. Not every training method suits every dog, and not every dog suits every person. If you have felt that the whole training course has been a constant battle and you have not achieved what you hoped for, you might seek further professional help from your dog training club or vet.

Finding Out More

There are countless publications on the market covering every aspect of dog ownership – from the dog's health to advanced competition sports. Some of these books are not available from high street stores, but can be obtained through specialist stockists – many of these have trade stands at championship breed shows. A visit to such a show will give you the opportunity to browse through the selection before making a purchase. The choice is staggering, but remember however many books you read, unless you enjoy regular training and make it fun for you and your dog, you will never reach your, or your dog's, full potential.

A Dog Is for Life

It cannot be stressed enough, but if you are thinking of buying and training a new dog, avoid the impulse to purchase a pet because of beautifully-groomed and well-behaved dogs in advertisemenst, or "my friend's dog had puppies and they were so cute." This can so often lead to disaster.

Index

Page numbers in italics denote caption.

Acknowledgments

To Robin Neillands and to Beauregard for getting us going. (KINSEY & Harrison)

Index by Patricia Hymans.
Additional photography by Stella Smyth (pages 22, 23, 26, 51 and 125)

The Authors would like to thank the following people and dogs who helped in the production of this book (and apologies to anyone we've left out):

Tracy Morgan Animal Photography for her expertise. Moss End Garden Centre Ltd for the loan of all the training equipment. Straid Veterinary Hospital for the use of the Vet's Coat. For modelling Thomas Kinsey, Stephanie and Adam Carpenter. Frank Gray and Travis (Australian Shepherd Dog), Mindy Gittoes and Conker (Welsh Terrier.), Kathy, Emma and Sophie Chapman and Rosie (Labrador), Lisa White and Woody (Golden Retriever), Caroline Graham and Piglet (Cross-breed), Sue Cragie and Kip and Zena (Rhodesian Ridgeback). Lady Huntingdon and her puppy (Australian Cattle Dog) Our own dogs: German Shepherd Dogs Chaos (Olderhill Abeth at Sarsway Companion Dog Excellent, Utility Dog Excellent, Working Dog Excellent, Tracking Dog Excellent), Hudson (Sarsway Arak Companion Dog Excellent, Utility Dog Excellent, Working Dog Excellent, Tracking Dog Excellent), Mallik (Sarsway Ardent Companion Dog Excellent, Utility Dog Excellent, Working Dog Excellent, Tracking Dog), Logan (Conquell Qwango). Australian Cattle Dogs – Smoky (Morrow Blue Aborigine Companion Dog Excellent, Utility Dog Excellent, Working Dog Excellent, Tracking Dog Excellent), Kynie (Warrigal Blue Kookynie at Morrow Companion Dog, Utility Dog Excellent, Working Dog), Mulga (Morrow Red Chakola), Skippy.

FURTHER READING
We have found the following books to be very helpful in trying to be at one with our dogs:

The Family Dog by John Holmes, (Popular Dogs Publishing Co, 1975)
How to Own a Sensible Dog by Joyce Stranger, (Corgi Books, 1981)
Don't Shoot the Dog by Karen Pryor, (Bantam Books, 1985)
Tracking Dog by Glen Johnson, (Arner Publications, 1975)
How to be Your Dog's Best Friend by the Monks of New Skete, (Little, Brown & Co. Publishing, 1978)